WINGS FOR SALE

To David,

Very best wishes,

Barry Wheeler

First Edition

Published in 2016 by

Woodfield Publishing Ltd
www.woodfieldpublishing.co.uk

ISBN 978-1-84683-180-5

Printed and bound in England

Typesetting & page design: Nic Pastorius
Cover design: Klaus Schaffer

Source document
Wings for Sale by Barry Lloyd (final) X8

Wings for Sale

*Worldwide experiences of an
aircraft salesman 1981-94*

BARRY LLOYD

Woodfield

Woodfield Publishing Ltd

Bognor Regis ~ West Sussex ~ England ~ PO21 5EL
tel 01243 821234 ~ **e/m** info@woodfieldpublishing.co.uk

Interesting and informative books on a variety of subjects

For full details of all our published titles, visit our website at
www.woodfieldpublishing.co.uk

My original plan, when I left school, was to join the Merchant Navy, not just because I was born and bred in a major seaport, but because I have always been fascinated by foreign lands, their people, climate and way of life.

*However, living next to an airport eventually changed all that. In the days when you could wander into hangars and talk to people about what they were doing, I did just that and met two very inspirational people, **Cliff Watson** and **Cedric Flood**. Thus began my interest and subsequently my career, in aviation.*

Along the way I have been fortunate enough to meet many other supportive and interesting people.

Aviation is a fascinating industry, much of which the public hears little of, except when things go wrong, but behind it there are tens of thousands of dedicated people in all parts of the industry who keep it ticking over 24 hours a day, seven days a week.

There have been a few moments of regret, but only a few and I wouldn't have changed it for the world.

Barry Lloyd, *November 2016*

How many people does it take to sell an aircraft? The BAe and SATA teams assemble for the handover of their new aircraft prior to delivery. [Avro Heritage Museum]

Contents

The 146 demonstrator arrives in Sao Paulo's downton airport during the Air Bridge campaign. [Author]

Introduction

Most people, when they step on board an aircraft, simply see it as a means of getting them from A to B as quickly and safely as possible, which is perfectly understandable, because that is precisely what it is designed to do. I very much doubt whether anyone ever wonders why the operator chose that particular type, that colour scheme, that layout.

The business of selling aeroplanes has always been something of a dark art but they certainly don't sell themselves, hence the need for a knowledgeable sales force. From the point of view of the airline operators, the task of choosing which aircraft to buy and how it will fit into their particular fleet is both complicated and time-consuming.

All aircraft manufacturers, large or small, employ sales teams to travel around the world talking to operators, keeping them updated about their latest models and innovations and making sure that when an order is being considered, they are included in the deliberations. For all manufacturers, the business is huge and winning or losing a large order can have a dramatic effect on company finances, production planning and the job security of the workforce in the factories.

The competition to win a significant order can be intense and such is the level of importance placed on them that frequently national governments become involved and exert influence to secure a deal, even if the prospective purchaser is an independent operator. The determination to win a lucrative contract can often be so great that competing manufacturers will resort to underhand methods in order to gain an advantage over the competition.

Once the operator has chosen the aircraft they want to purchase, the contract negotiations will take place. These often involve complex financing, insurance and legal considerations and are always conducted in the knowledge that the competition is still 'waiting in the wings' (pardon the pun), ready to pounce if negotiations should falter. It is against such a background that most deals are done. This is rarely reported in the media and few books have been written about it, so it seems appropriate to set down my own experiences, both good and bad, in this rather unusual business.

The sales campaigns detailed in this book cover two specific periods. From 1981 to 1988 I worked for the commercial aircraft division of what was then called **British Aerospace**, based at Woodford near Manchester and later at Stevenage. The aircraft we were selling were the **BAe 748**, the **ATP** and the **Bae 146**. My allocated territories were South America, the Caribbean and parts of Europe.

Our principal competitors were the Dutch **Fokker F 27** which, like the 748, had two Rolls-Royce engines, but was high-winged and because of this, the fuselage was much nearer the ground than the 748. The French **ATR 42** was very new on the scene and was not introduced into service until 1985, but this didn't stop the Toulouse-based ATR manufacturers from competing for every deal. The ATR 42 and its bigger stable-mate, the **ATR 72** were also high-winged.

De Havilland Canada (DHC) also built a 48-seat aircraft known as the **Dash 7**. This was a four-engined high-winged aircraft originally designed and built by DHC, but following the sale of DHC to **Boeing** in 1986 and the subsequent refusal of **Air Canada** to buy Boeing aircraft for its fleet, the jigs and other specialised equipment for its manufacture were destroyed, following which Boeing immediately put DHC up for sale, placing the company in jeopardy. It was eventually acquired by **Bombardier** Aerospace in 1992, by which time the Dash 8, with two engines and a high wing, which had been originally designed and produced by DHC was already established in the marketplace. However, it did not enter service until 1985 and thus was less of a competitor with the earlier campaigns.

With the **Bae 146** the only serious competitors were the **Boeing 737** and the **Fokker 100**, both twin-engined low-winged aircraft initially designed to hold about 100 passengers.

The aircraft I was responsible for were the **BAe 748**, the **BAe 146** (which in its various versions could seat up to 130 people) and the **BAe ATP**.

The **BAe 748** (or *Avro* as it was better known, after the name of its original designer, A.V. Roe) was built in Manchester, with the wings and fuselage being constructed at Chadderton in north Manchester and then taken by road to be completed and test-flown at the final assembly plant and airfield at Woodford, south of the city. A total of 380 aircraft were sold to countries as diverse as the Marshall Islands and Madagascar. Both civil and military versions were produced. **Hindustan Aviation** built 89 of these aircraft under licence in India.

The **BAe** (originally HS) **146** was initially built at Hatfield but when Hatfield closed in 1993, production was moved to Woodford. It was produced in three different sizes with the largest, the 146-300 typically having 120 seats. A total of 387 of these aircraft were sold around the world, to countries as diverse as Bhutan and The Faroe Islands. A *VIP version* was also available and was supplied to several heads of state, including Queen Elizabeth II in the UK.

The **BAe ATP** (Advanced Turbo-Prop) was an up-dated version of the BAe 748 with 64 seats and a flight deck equipped with electronic systems. It made its first flight in 1987. The ATP was less successful than its predecessor, with only 64 examples being built. Many of those still flying operate as freighters, particularly in Scandinavia.

At a later point in my career, between 1990 and 1994, I joined the *Corporate Jets* division of British Aerospace, which was responsible for manufacturing the **BAe 125** (originally made by **de**

Havilland and later **Hawker Siddeley**). It was commonly known in many countries as *The Hawker*. Originally designed as an eight-seater business jet, over the years many design changes took place, culminating in the 125-1000, a 12-seat aircraft with a range of 3,000 nautical miles. Almost 1,700 of these aircraft were built during its 50-year lifespan. As with the 748, operators included large corporations, governments, air forces around the world and, of course, numerous private owners. Its main competitors were the **Bombardier Challenger 600**, the **Dassault Falcon** the **Learjet 25** and the **Cessna Citation**.

This then is the background to my involvement in the business of selling aircraft.

Naturally I have chosen the more interesting campaigns I was involved with as examples, in order to give a flavour of what selling aircraft can entail, the intention being to offer an insight into what, at times, can be an extremely frustrating, but at others an extremely rewarding business. The campaigns are presented in chronological order although some overlapped, which was by design, because South America is a long way from the UK and much bigger than most British people imagine. For example, a flight from Caracas to Buenos Aires would typically take about seven hours – the same as from London to Dubai. Therefore it made sense, wherever possible, to combine campaigns and use our visits to the region to maximum advantage.

DEMONSTRATION FLIGHTS

THERE ARE MANY REFERENCES in the book to *demonstration flights*, so it seems appropriate to explain exactly what they involve. It is common knowledge that air shows are held all over the world – Farnborough, Paris, Dubai, Singapore, etc – which give aircraft manufacturers an opportunity to show off their latest models. Representatives from the airline operators come to the shows to meet other members of the aviation community and exchange news and views. Aircraft are demonstrated executing manoeuvres they would never perform in everyday operation, to impress visiting dignitaries and show off their capabilities (but, of course, no passengers are on board at the time).

Air shows are a great opportunity to showcase new aircraft but are not an environment in which sales are actually made. The real demonstrations take place in the country where the prospective customer is based. This is because they will want to see that the aircraft they are considering acquiring can operate safely and efficiently in local conditions and to and from the airports on their route network.

Investing in a fleet or even just one aircraft involves a lot of time and money and an operator may keep an aircraft for up to 20 years, so clearly any purchase is a long-term commitment. If you consider that an aircraft like the 748 cost 1,000 times the price of a top-of-the-range saloon car, you would certainly be looking for a demonstration before you decided whether or not to buy.

In the case of airlines, demonstrations normally only took place after 'all the numbers had been run', in other words a full feasibility study, which would typically include the cost of ownership, maintenance costs, fuel burns, flight times on each sector, etc., to demonstrate how that particular aircraft might fit into their fleet. The manufacturer will assist in this by providing proposed schedules for the sectors based on their current timetable, usually with the planning department in a large airline, together with likely maintenance intervals and costs, a support package and a delivery schedule, particularly if more than one aircraft is involved, so that they can be efficiently integrated into the fleet.

If the aircraft was required to land on unprepared runways, and the manufacturer claimed that it was particularly adept at this, you would want to see this with your own eyes and check the manufacturer's claims before parting with any money.[1] These demonstrations were not undertaken lightly, however, since considerable costs were involved, not least in flying the demonstration aircraft to where they were required. Such flights only took place when serious intent was being shown by the customer.

The 125, 146 and 748 were all capable of being fitted with 'rough field kits'. This meant that they could be operated into airfields which did not have solid runway surfaces, for example grass or graded soil or even fine gravel, and consisted largely of additional protection to the undercarriage and the areas around it. This was a unique selling point, as many airfields in less developed countries had such surfaces and these airfields were often the only link with the outside world. Such airfields were often deliberately chosen during demonstration flights in order to maximise our chances of selling the aircraft. Most of our competitors' aircraft could not achieve this without substantial work, weight and cost being added to their aircraft during production.

In the case of larger long-haul aircraft, flying the demonstration aircraft from the manufacturer's base to the airline's base is not particularly difficult, even if it is a long way away. Such aircraft are designed to fly long distances and with only a few passengers on board (i.e. the sales team) can fly much further than they could in airline service. However, for smaller, short-haul aircraft, this can be something of a challenge. They are not designed to fly half-way around the world without stopping and are not as fast as long-haul jets, so the whole process of flying the demonstration aircraft to

---

[1] Unlike those of most of BAe's direct competitors, the aircraft I was selling were specifically designed to operate out of short, unprepared airstrips, anywhere in the world.

the country in which the operator is based can require a considerable amount of planning.

In the case of the BAe 748 and 146, these aircraft were designed to fly sectors of up to three hours with passengers. Thus, if we had to take them to South America, for example, it would take us many days to make the journey. We would normally follow a fixed pattern: Iceland, Greenland, Labrador and then Washington (our headquarters in the US), where we could perform maintenance, pick up additional spare parts (if required) and plan the rest of the route.

From there it would usually be a stop in Fort Lauderdale (because it was quieter and smaller than Miami International). If our destination was the Caribbean, we'd usually use Antigua as the base, because the operator there, LIAT, had 748s and thus spares, if they were required. If it was South America, it would be on to Jamaica via the Cuban corridor, perhaps a quick stop for refuelling, or directly to Panama and further down the east or west coast of South America, as required, with the prevailing weather conditions both en-route and at destination being taken into account.

Of course, once a purchased aircraft was ready for delivery, it would follow a similar route. If it was going to the Far East, a typical routing would be: Crete, the United Arab Emirates, Mumbai (or somewhere further east, depending on the winds and weather), then Bangkok or Singapore, depending on the ultimate destination.

In the following pages I have described some of the highs and lows I encountered during my years working on aircraft sales campaigns. No two campaigns were alike, some took longer than others, but they were always complicated. A typical contract, including leasing, insurance, maintenance, training, ongoing spares, delivery, colour scheme and other negotiable items could run to five or six volumes. Every page had to be initialled by both the buyer and the seller.

Once the paperwork was back in the office, the customer had to make the initial payment, following which allocations for the aircraft would to be made on the production line and training courses for the crews and engineers organised. Often it would be a year or more before the shiny new aircraft was towed out of the hangar for its first test flight, by which time the salesman responsible for that deal would probably be somewhere far away, tracking down the next deal...

The 748 Coastguarder during a refuelling stop at Narsarsuaq, Greenland. This picture was taken in July - note the ice floes in the bay! [Author]

Curse of the Coastguarder (1981)

We had tried on a number of occasions to interest the Ministry of Defence in other potential versions of the 748. They had already taken delivery of the Andover, a stretched version of the 748 with a ramp at the rear, but the design department had come up with an aircraft with a 'chin' radar, based on the fact that there was much talk at the time of Economic Exclusion Zones and how they would be policed. The aircraft would also carry additional equipment, such as cameras, sophisticated navigation equipment and a sonar buoy launch chute.

In 1981, the Ministry of Defence was still deeply in love with the Nimrod, a maritime reconnaissance aircraft, which was being re-built from old Comet airframes. They wanted to use it for both inshore and offshore maritime patrol but we felt that the Coast-gaurder, being more manoeuvrable at lower speeds, was better suited to the inshore work, leaving the Nimrod to perform the longer offshore duties. The Ministry had little appetite for this idea but we were not to be put off so easily.

Our Chief Test Pilot hatched a cunning plan. As part of what was then known as The Greenham Common Air Show, an event called 'Sea Search 81' had been organised. Invitations to partake in this event had been issued to the military in countries all over the world. He sent off an application form, half-expecting a refusal, but in fact his application was happily accepted and he now had to explain to the MD of the company what he had done. As it happened, the MD was quite amenable to the idea, so the next task was to pick the crew and make all the arrangements, because the competition was going to last for a week.

Although the Chief Test Pilot had put a good crew together, we were up against regular professionals from all the other teams and realistically we had only taken part to bring the Coastguarder to everyone's attention and to try to reinforce our case to the MoD. So it was a great surprise to all concerned when we won the competition! On the back of this, we began to receive enquiries from a number of countries about it and in June 1981 we set off for Ecuador and Peru with stops in Jamaica, Trinidad, Colombia and Mexico, to demonstrate its capabilities.

During the Falklands conflict one item which had little, if any, mention in the UK was the fact that many countries in Latin America have offshore possessions, in the form of small islands. The Galapagos are well-known and belong to Ecuador but Colombia has a group of islands in the Caribbean 750km (470m) north-west of the coast of Colombia and just 230km (140m) off the coast of Nicaragua, called the San Andres Islands. Nicaragua itself has the Corn Islands, Honduras has the Bay Islands and so on.

The Falklands conflict was watched with great interest by these nations, not least because in most cases their territorial integrity was – or had been – in dispute and they were afraid that if Argentina did take the Falklands (Malvinas), other nations might be tempted to attempt copycat incursions. It was widely reported locally at the time that the Nicaraguan Air Force had made a number of low flights over the San Andres Islands. Their claim of sovereignty over the islands has been running for almost 100 years. Whilst few, if any of them would openly admit it, there were large sighs of relief when the British finally rid the islands of the invaders, thus setting an example to any would-be attacker.

As usual, we took the scenic route via Iceland and Greenland, but this time, because of the radome under the forward fuselage, the cruising speed of the aircraft was slightly reduced and the fuel consumption slightly increased and so the flight planning had to be done very carefully.

We departed from Woodford, our factory and airfield near Manchester in the afternoon and headed towards Reykjavik for the night-stop. Reykjavik was a good night stop because the hotel was actually part of the airport and as capitals go, it was small and compact, thus it was a quick and easy journey into town.

We headed for the first bar we could find. We walked in and ordered our drinks, only to be told that they did not serve alcohol on a Thursday night, which we initially thought was some kind of joke, but apparently there had been numerous problems with heavy drinking and the government of the day had decreed that there had to be an alcohol-free day. A mental note was made amongst us to remember not to transit Reykjavik on Thursdays in future!

The following morning we would then head across to Greenland, where another of our regular transit stops was Narsarsuaq in Greenland. The airfield had been built during WWII as a transit point for the US Air Force and was initially known as Bluie West One. It is not an easy airport at which to land, because it lies near the end of a fjord and it is important to make a right turn before you reach the end.

At that time, there was little in the way of navigation equipment, but helpfully there was a red sunken trawler which lay in the fjord just before the right turn. There was always fuel available, but the weather was subject to sudden changes and there were few options for a diversion, principally because once the weather closes in in Greenland, there are very few airports available.

Our alternative in this case was Sondestrom, but the problem with that airport is that its more northerly position means that the weather can often be worse than it is in Narsarsuaq. Therefore the weather had to be checked carefully before leaving Reykjavik. If in doubt, we would wait until the weather cleared before attempting the Reykjavik–Narsarsuaq sector. From there, we would head to eastern Canada for another night stop. This meant that the most difficult part of the transit would be done in daytime.

On this occasion, we stopped in Sept Iles in Quebec Province, with Goose Bay in Labrador as our alternate. From here, we headed on to Washington for a technical and fuel stop and to plan the remainder of the journey. The fact that we had an office in Washington made this so much easier. We then headed down to Fort Lauderdale for the next night-stop.

After taking off from Fort Lauderdale and on the way between there and Jamaica, the fine weather gave us the ideal opportunity to test the equipment on board the aircraft. Having received permission from air traffic control, we flew around for a while, using the Searchwater radar, a similar system to that which was being used on the Nimrod, to identify the ships and then circled around them using the Agiflite camera to record their positions, we then were given permission to descend over the Caribbean and decided to pick out a few ocean-going vessels and especially to use the camera, which had 70mm film and could also include the time, latitude and longitude on whatever images were taken, thus eliminating any possibility of denial by the ship's crew. There were certainly a few surprised merchant and fishing ships' crews that day, but the equipment worked very well and we were confident of being able to make a good impression to the potential customers.

We eventually reached Peru and set up a demonstration flight to the Peruvian Navy. Peru has a large fishing fleet and they are understandably protective of their waters. Fish meal (based mainly on anchovies) is a very important export.

Timekeeping has never been a strong point in Latin America. Indeed, for anyone to actually arrive on time is generally known as *tiempo ingles* – English time. The Peruvians, true to this tradition, turned up two hours after the departure time we had agreed. We were parked some distance away from the main terminal at Lima's Jorge Chavez airport in the military area, with its huge expanse of concrete.

Although we had arrived at the beginning of the Peruvian winter it was unusually hot, with the temperature around the 25C mark, and the reflection of the sun from the concrete, plus the fact that the aircraft was camouflaged, made the wait rather unpleasant. We had a GPU (Ground Power Unit) plugged into the aircraft, but there is only so much power available and it doesn't normally run to air conditioning.

Eventually the great and good of the Peruvian Navy arrived, we gave them a briefing on what we proposed to do, then took off and set course for a point about 250km west of Lima. We climbed out, initially to avoid the normal commercial traffic and then began our descent. As we levelled out at a few hundred feet above sea level we were surprised at just how clear the water was. So clear, in fact, that we could see shoals of manta rays languidly making their way further out into the Pacific.

The Peruvians had long had a close relationship with the Soviet Union and most of their equipment, both aviation and naval, was of Soviet origin and whilst we had nothing which could be classed as 'secret' on board we were a little wary of their interest, because previous attempts to sell anything vaguely military to them had been rebuffed.

The exercise was carried out to everyone's apparent satisfaction, the usual polite formalities were observed, but we never heard any more from them, nor did they acquire a maritime reconnaissance aircraft.

Our next stop was Ecuador. The Ecuadorian Air Force had a number of 748s in its inventory, including one which operated for the Presidential flight. The main base for the Ecuadorian Air Force is Quito, the capital. The airport at Quito sits at 9,228ft (2,813m) above sea level but despite its' height and because it is almost exactly on the Equator, has a high ambient temperature.

The air is thin at that altitude and approach speeds must be managed very carefully, as must the landing weight. Our calculations for the landing weight were fine but unfortunately our approach speed was a little too fast, which meant that we landed rather heavily and burst two tyres in the process. The fire tenders were called out to follow us onto the military ramp at the airport. Naturally, this was rather embarrassing but made more embarrassing by the fact that, unknown to us, the Ecuadorian Air Force had set up a reception committee, together with a full marching band, to welcome our arrival. It was also being filmed for that night's TV news programme.

The burst tyres were ignored for a while as we went through the motions of the reception but, once everyone had left, we set about the task of replacing the tyres. The Ecuadorians were extremely diplomatic about the whole business and little was said about the incident. Fortunately, being a 748 operator, the Air Force had all the equipment and qualified help we needed to do the tyre changes, but even so, this activity is not to be recommended at an elevation of nine thousand feet! Once everything had been completed it was off to the hotel for a shower and a few cold beers.

The following morning we took off for Guayaquil, on the Pacific coast, which is the main base for the Ecuadorian Navy. Again, we flew out in perfect weather conditions over the Pacific towards, but not with the intention of landing in, the Galapagos Islands, overflying an area where it was known that foreign fishing vessels often illegally fished for shrimp. Shrimp-fishing is very big business in Ecuador and a significant amount is exported, even to Europe, earning useful foreign exchange. Several unauthorised fishing vessels were sighted off the coast and we were able to record the information for their records. Again, we saw shoals of manta rays, the combination of low flying and crystal clear water giving us excellent views, both above and below the water.

The Ecuadorian Navy were very impressed with what were able to show them and we returned to Guayaquil for a debrief. After this, and upon returning to the aircraft, we discovered that one of the more temperamental pieces of equipment on board was running short of liquid nitrogen, which was required for cooling. We asked the local agent if he knew where we could obtain some, but he was unable to help. At the time, Ecuador printed an excellent version of 'Yellow Pages' and after a few enquiries around the airport, we eventually found a copy in one of the offices and I began looking for suppliers of industrial gases. I found one and called them to ask whether we could purchase a small amount of liquid nitrogen. They happily agreed, so we went back to the aircraft, retrieved the bottle, which resembled a very large vacuum flask, and took a taxi to the plant. The taxi driver was rather sceptical at first, seeing the engineer with a large flask and a blanket, but after a couple of attempts, we found the huge distribution plant and, without further ado, the bottle was filled. None of our reassurances put the taxi-driver's mind to rest however, because he cast frequent nervous glances over his shoulder as we headed back to the airport.

We took off back to Quito that evening, landed without incident and proceeded to the hotel.

One of the other contenders for the aircraft was Trinidad & Tobago, who as it happened, already had four 748s in operation. These were used to connect the two islands, because the airport, known at that time at that time as Crown Point, had a short runway and could not accept large aircraft. Thus the Coastguarder would fit in well with their operations. Being just 11km off the coast of Venezuela, and in an area rich in sea life and smuggling, the islands suffered frequent incursions from fishing vessels from other countries, not all of them local to the area. The demonstration took place to the Defence Force and they were clearly interested in such an aircraft, however, they eventually two much smaller US-built aircraft.

The next stop was Colombia, where we took the aircraft to the northern coast and the port of Barranquilla, which was well-known for its smuggling activities. The Colombians were getting help from several navies, including the UK to try to combat the drug and other smuggling, but such was the ingenuity of the smugglers and huge area of the Caribbean in which they were operating, that it was extremely difficult to keep track of their activities. Again, the Colombians, as operators of the 748 thought the Coastguarder a good match, but, as ever, money for such a useful tool in the fight against the smugglers was not forthcoming from the government.

From there, the aircraft went on to Jamaica and Mexico, although I had to stay behind to attend to other business and did not take part in those demonstrations. Eventually, the aircraft headed back to Woodford via the US and the original outbound route.

Unfortunately, we never sold any Coastguarders. The reasons we were given were that it was too big for their requirements, primarily because the equipment they required would be more expensive than the aircraft itself, although the equipment they could put on board was entirely bespoke. The aircraft, although called the Coastguarder, was actually a muti-role aircraft which could be used for paratrooping or carrying military equipment, always with the knowledge that it could perform from unprepared strips.

Ironically, the demonstrator aircraft we used was eventually sold to the Sri Lankan Air Force, and now sits in a semi-derelict condition near a disputed airport site in southern Sri Lanka.

The LIAT Lark (1981–85)

I n 1981 **Leeward Islands Air Transport** (LIAT) decided that their fleet of 748s needed replacing. The 748s they had were Series 2As, and several of them had given 16 years of good service, but the relatively short sectors and the salt-laden sea air had taken their toll on both the airframes and the engines. British-based Court Line had owned LIAT since 1971, but when Court Line filed for bankruptcy in 1974, it was taken over by a consortium of no less than 12 Caribbean governments, most of which were, by now, independent of the UK. The airline had applied to the EEC (as it then was) for funding under a Regional Development Grant. This meant that the whole purchasing process had to go through a full competition programme via a bid system administered by Brussels. Only companies which were based in EEC countries could apply, which we believed meant that only ourselves and Fokker of the Netherlands could submit bids. Aerospatiale of France were still in the design stage with their competitor, the ATR 42, so it was not admitted into the competition. The bids were submitted and then the fun began...

There was a problem. EEC competition rules stated that all competition bids had to have three bidders, which was difficult because there was no other manufacturer of 50-seat aircraft within the Community. Of course, they didn't have to tell us who the third bidder would be and they didn't! It was only on a later visit to LIAT when I saw the technical specifications for the Canadian-built De Havilland Dash 7 on the CEO's desk that I realised who the 'third man' would be. LIAT were as mystified as we were, but they had been given no explanation either, presumably on the basis that they weren't actually paying for the goods! The EEC had declared that at least nine of the countries involved in the consortium had to support the final decision, otherwise the bid would be declared void.

We were offering the **BAe 748-2B** series, an improved version of the aircraft they were currently operating, which, was able to offer better airfield performance on some of the shorter runways. Fokker were offering the **F-27** which had never really operated in the Caribbean, so they were naturally keen to get a foothold in that market. DHC, having had the carrot dangled in front of them, grasped it with both hands. We learnt later that because some of the equipment on it was British it had been admitted into the process – such were the crazy decisions of the EEC, even then! We learned later that Fokker complained formally to the EEC about DHC's inclusion, but to no avail.

The first thing we had to do was assess the value of the existing aircraft, in order to put a financial offer in place. This was complicated because one of the aircraft had a large freight door (LFD) and was only three years old at the time, although it was planned to replace the whole fleet. Because of the extra weight associated with LFDs, this particular aircraft could not operate into some of the more restricted airfields, such as St Vincent and Grenada. LIAT very rarely used the large freight door anyway, so they wanted to get rid of this aircraft first. Given the nature of LIAT's operation, all their planes had high hours and landings, but nevertheless were well-maintained and thus sought-after, particularly in less-developed nations. Being the OEM, BAe were thus able to offer better trade-in values. Because of their relatively remote location in those days, LIAT had a huge spares holding, which they would have to dispose of if they bought another type.

It is perhaps worth mentioning that there was only a twice weekly service to Antigua from the UK in those days. If we had to travel on other days, it was either via Miami or one of the French Caribbean islands, usually with an overnight stay involved, whichever route we took. The French route was interesting, because upon producing my passport following a flight from Paris to Guadeloupe I was told by the customs officer that it was not required.

"*Monsieur, vous ne pas besoin d'un passeport, vous êtes encore en France*", I was told.

It has always amazed me how France has held on to its colonial territories. Dutch Guyana became Suriname after independence and British Guiana became Guyana, but French Guiana is still going strong. Britain still has some *overseas territories*, as it calls them, including a few Caribbean islands, but not nearly as many as our neighbours across the Channel.

We submitted an initial bid, which in turn was followed by an EEC delegation visit to Antigua to assess LIAT's requirements and operation. At this point it became apparent, that for various reasons, several of the consortium members were not in favour of the 748. DHC, having learned of this, then began to play the politics game. The consortium members were all part of the Commonwealth, as indeed is Canada, but of course Canada is not a member of the EEC, so they were able to offer regional improvement grants of their own to some of the islands on the basis that they in turn would support the DHC bid, though the two were not of course connected. The islands who were not supporting the bid were Grenada (of whom more later), St Vincent, Dominica and St Lucia. Guyana, although a member of the consortium, had no interest whatsoever in the process, since at the time, LIAT didn't fly to Guyana anyway.

ST VINCENT

LIKE MANY ISLANDS IN the Eastern Caribbean, St Vincent is quite hilly, and there aren't many places where you can build a useful runway. A site had been found in **Arnos Vale** but at a rather awkward spot, because it was in a valley and also ran into the sea at one end and had houses and larger buildings at the other. The combination of these factors led on a number of occasions to the *crosswind component* to be *above limits* (i.e. too strong to attempt a landing) for the 748, which is saying something, because at 27kts this was significantly higher than all its competitors. In fact, the first time I flew into St Vincent, we were right on the limits and had to fly around for 15 minutes while we waited for the wind to drop! Apparently a new airport is being built NE of Arnos Vale with a 9,000ft runway. It is due to open in 2016. Politically, there had been arguments with the UK over independence, which had been achieved in 1979, so there was not a lot of love for the UK at the time I was there.

DOMINICA

DOMINICA (PRONOUNCED DOM-IN-EEKA AND not to be confused with the Dominican Republic) is also quite mountainous, but has two airports. One is named **Canefield** because it lies in what was once a large field of sugar cane, just to the south of a village called Massacre (!). The runway is about 3,000ft long with a tarmac surface. Despite being the smaller of the two airfields it is more frequently used because of its close proximity to the capital, Roseau. The other airfield, then called **Melville Hall** (a rather cool name for an airport, I always thought) was in the north of the island. At the time both airports were daylight-only operation. Although the 748 could land at Melville Hall, it's big disadvantage was it's distance from Roseau and the poor road connections over the mountains. At the time, the Prime Minister of the island was a redoubtable lady called Eugenia Charles, who was 64 when I first met her. She was sharp as a knife but very critical of LIAT, which had led her to the 'no' camp.

ST LUCIA

ANOTHER MOUNTAINOUS ISLAND WITH two airfields, **Vigie** and **Hewanorra**. Again, LIAT used Vigie as it was nearer to Castries, the capital. Hewanorra is used for long-haul flights from Europe and North America. Perhaps because of its French connections, St Lucia did not support the 748 in the bid process.

GRENADA

It wasn't so much that Grenada didn't support the bid. They had a few problems of their own at the time. The lone airport, called **Pearls** was another daylight-only operation, with mountains at one end of the runway and the Caribbean at the other, which allowed landings only in one direction and take-offs in the other. Significant flying skills were required for these operations, as was proved during the Grenada crisis, when a Russian-built Cuban aircraft came to grief on the airfield. The last time I looked, it was still there.

Given that the island has some excellent beaches and spectacular inland scenery, the government wanted to encourage more tourism into what was, by any standards, an economically poor island, famous at the time as a major provider of the world's nutmeg.

Unable to find funding for a new airport from the usual sources, its government had turned to Cuba. The Cubans had agreed to build a civil airport with a 9,000ft runway. The head of state at the time had strong Socialist leanings and Cubans were brought in to do the construction work. The US, paranoid as ever, saw this as nothing less than the installation of a useful military landing strip for Soviet aircraft en-route to and from Cuba, despite the fact that the fuel tanks were built above ground – something you would never do with a military installation. The whole business resulted in a lot of political soul-searching on both sides of the Atlantic and a temporary falling-out between Thatcher and Reagan.

Naturally, the eyes of the Grenadan government were on this situation rather than the bid, so it was time to hatch a cunning plan. We spoke to the High Commissions[1] on several islands, who arranged meetings with the governments of dissenting islands.

---

[1] If a country is a member of the Commonwealth, it has a High Commission rather than an embassy.

So it was time to do a bit of island-hooping as part of the campaign. We went on a tour of the dissenting islands in a chartered small plane. It wasn't entirely successful, but then the other option was to do nothing and allow things to become worse.

A couple of LIAT directors travelled with us and we were able to meet their nominated directors on other islands. One meeting which sticks in my mind was with their representative in Grenada. He was serving coffee on his terrace which, coincidentally, overlooked the runway at Pearls airport.

"Help yourselves to sugar; it's not Cuban, honestly!" he said.

We also managed to convince one High Commissioner, who had been supporting the Fokker bid (apparently because it had Rolls-Royce engines and a British undercarriage!), not realising that the 748 was built in the UK and had very little foreign content. Clearly a knowledge of British industry is not a huge factor when appointing our diplomats, despite the fact that he admitted to having flown regularly on the 748.

The next activity involved almost weekly commuting to Brussels to answer questions about performance, both of the existing 748s and those proposed, plus dealing with the absurd political red tape just to keep the bid moving through the system.

Over a period of about six months, Fokker, somewhat to our surprise, was eliminated in favour of DHC, who had played the short take-off and landing capabilities of the Dash 7 quite convincingly to the EEC and the islands with smaller airfields (whilst failing to point out the increased fuel and maintenance costs of a four-engine aircraft versus a two-engine one). The EEC were not concerned about the operational costs however, since they would not be paying them – they were simply funding the cost of the replacement aircraft.

The next stage in the competition was a demonstration of the aircraft we were offering. As it happened, we had already planned a demo trip for Colombia and Venezuela so it was fairly easy to slot in a trip to Antigua on the way back – or so we thought!

Of course DHC were doing the same and we were up against them on a totally different bid in Colombia – supplying two 48-seat aircraft to fly coal miners to an area called Cerrejon – a region so remote that it could only be reached by air at the time. The coal was removed by a freight line. The Cerrejon bid was interesting, but because we were so busy with the LIAT bid, we almost ran out of time to submit the bid. The company handling the bid was based in San Francisco and the documents had to be handed in personally by the bidder. One of my colleagues thus got the opportunity to fly Concorde to New York, where he was promptly upgraded to First Class on the basis that he'd just flown the Atlantic on Concorde. Incidentally, the mine is still going strong and I believe it supplies much of the coal to the UK these days.

For this demo, I needed to be there in advance in order to plan the itinerary and so I was spared the usual six-day transit in a 748 from our factory near Manchester to Bogotá. The 748 was built for short-haul routes and crossing the Atlantic became something of a challenge for such an aircraft, involving many stops and routing via Iceland, Greenland, Canada and the east coast of the US, although I am pleased to say that we achieved it many times without any major incidents.

We did not a have a demonstrator aircraft available at the time, so we had pulled a production aircraft off the line, put a basic blue colour scheme on it and sent it on its' way. The first demo stop was in a town called Mitú in order to do a demonstration to a cargo airline based deep in the jungle, not far from the Brazilian border. Later we took it to Cerrejon to demonstrate the abilities of the 748 to operate from unprepared runways. We then crossed to Venezuela and did a demonstration in Isla Margarita in Venezuela, which for a brief time later was very popular with British holidaymakers.

While the demos were taking place on Isla Margarita, I was tasked with filing the flight plan to Antigua for the LIAT demo the following day. The first problem was that *antigua* in Spanish (none of the staff in the airport spoke English and, as became quickly evident, were not well versed in Caribbean geography), means 'old' (or indeed 'antique'). So here's this guy saying he wants to file a flight plan to somewhere they've never heard of called 'old'. I tried another tack, but they practically rolled on the floor laughing when I mentioned Barbados. *Barba* in Spanish, you will not be surprised to learn, means beard and Barbados means *bearded men*. So here's this crazy Gringo who wants to take an aircraft they've never seen before to two islands, one called *Old* and the other called *Bearded Men*. It was like a scene from Monty Python!

Eventually I gave up, called our office in Washington and asked them to file the flight plan. However, we weren't finished yet. It appeared that despite the information I had been given, Isla Margarita in those days only had customs and immigration facilities on request. A formal request had to made for this, so the forms were completed and submitted. However, they would not approve them until they had a copy of the flight plan approval. I called Washington again to check whether the plan had been filed and accepted and spoke to the guy in the sales office, who I knew quite well.

"What island is this you're on – Devil's Island?" he asked.

After about two hours, we got confirmation that everything was set up for a departure the following morning, but not before 1000 because customs would not be available before then. After all that, it was straight back to the hotel for a few cold beers!

The following day we set off for Barbados and Antigua. The demos took place without incident and the demonstrator aircraft was flown back to Woodford to be sold immediately to a new operator. I always thought it was rather sad that having survived two transatlantic crossings and numerous difficult demonstration flights, the aircraft, in the hands of another operator, was written off whilst taking off on a flight from Stansted to Leeds. Fortunately there were no major injuries.

In the meantime, the EEC evaluation continued at a snail's pace. We visited the regional HQ of the EEC in Barbados, where we met the person in charge of transport policy. He was just about one of the most useless individuals I have ever met. He had no idea what was going on, and was even less interested. A few months later he was removed because of a scandal totally unconnected with the LIAT bid and replaced by an Irishman, which made life a whole lot easier!

By now it is late 1983 and the whole Grenada story has now reached a climax. The US was on the cusp of Operation 'Urgent Fury'. I was there a week before the invasion and again a couple of weeks afterwards and, apart from the Operation 'Eagle Claw' (the bungled hostage rescue in Iran) it must be one of the most ignominious episodes in recent US military history. They had only tourist maps, they attacked from the wrong side of the island, where they couldn't land, their communications equipment didn't work and they had to resort to making phone calls (reverse charge!) from phone boxes around the island to keep in touch with HQ. And all this for 7,000 troops to invade what was, in effect, an unarmed Caribbean Island.

The effect of this was for many of those in Brussels to believe that the whole of the Caribbean was about to go war with the US and there would be nothing left, so why bother to continue with the bid process? At this point we had to get our own government to put some pressure on the EEC, a task which Mrs Thatcher, as can be imagined, took to with gusto, though having to provide a brief for her on a subject as complex as that was one of the most difficult tasks I ever had.

Three months later and we were summoned to Brussels to hear the verdict of the EEC. We had won!

Apparently the Dash 7 had not given a very good account of itself, the F-27 had already been eliminated and they were persuaded by the fact that our aircraft was very similar to the ones which they already had and that this was the overall preference expressed by LIAT. DHC had their revenge however, by winning the Cerrejon coal contract.

It was now early 1984 and we had been working on this deal for almost three years. It was, of course, a standing joke on the office.

"You guys are really milking this Caribbean deal – I wonder why?" "Can I come with you to Antigua? Everyone else has been there!" "The suntan's starting to fade, when are you going back?" were typical comments. We allocated four aircraft off the line and then started looking for outlets for the aircraft we'd be taking in part-exchange. It didn't take long. The first aircraft quickly went to Air Inuit in Canada – this was the 'newest' one with the large freight door, clearly a useful selling point in this case. In fact, it was on its way back to Woodford when it was sold whilst still in transit, much to the consternation of the two pilots, who ended up taking a scheduled flight back from Montreal!

LIAT did not have a good reputation in the Caribbean: 'Luggage In Another Terminal', 'Lost Inbetween Antigua and Trinidad' and 'Languishing In Airport Terminals' are a few of the more printable suggestions for the meaning of its initials that I can remember. However, they had a good overall safety record when you consider their operation, particularly with the 748s, none of which ever suffered a serious accident in LIAT service. The Caribbean is not always as sunny as we imagine and we experienced several tropical rainstorms during our visits there, when the local airport was closed for most of the day. They developed very quickly, and Met forecasting not being as sophisticated as it is today, the storms often caught all concerned unawares.

Several of the other 748s taken in part-exchange went to Canada and one ultimately to Bengal, and remained in operation for more than 30 years.

SATENA Shenanigans (1981–85)

S ATENA, or to use its full title **Servicio Aeronavegacion a Territorios Nacionales** is based in Colombia and is some-thing of a cross between a domestic carrier and a social service. It was formed by the Colombian government to serve parts of the country which are normally accessible only by bus, or there are so few potential passengers that it would be uneconomical to operate as a commercial service. It is run as an arm of the Colombian Air Force – **Fuerza Aerea Colombiana (FAC)** – all the crews wear FAC uniforms and the whole passenger experience is rudimentary, to say the least.

Colombia is traversed by three mountain ranges, known locally as the *Cordillera* (backbone). This makes moving around the country very difficult and road journeys are lengthy and perilous. Typically, a flight from Bogotá to Medellin would take 45 minutes, whilst a similar bus journey could take up to 12 hours, usually involving traversing narrow unlit mountain roads at night. Because of this, it wasn't unusual for a bus accident to take place once a week, often resulting in the deaths of all on board. Anyone who has watched 'The Road of Death' on the TV show *Top Gear* will get some idea of the conditions, except that there are many such roads in Colombia.

Satena, despite having been set up by the government, did not receive the amount of funding its operations deserved. As a result, they frequently repossessed DC3s and DC4s which had been abandoned in remote airfields by drug-runners, brought them back to Bogotá, put them through a thorough check and repainted them. In fact one day when I was sitting in the boss's office at the corner of the hangar, a WWII era four-engined DC4 taxied in – on three engines! It carried no registration, but was flown by Satena pilots and had been recovered from a jungle location.

Latin America is grossly under-reported in the UK, unless there are football matches being played there. Colombia, for example, is the same size as South Africa, but it is difficult to imagine just how much drug production and smuggling was taking place in Colombia in the early 80s. Because of the large number of remote areas and their temperate climate, drug production was extremely easy and far more financially rewarding than growing coffee or pineapples. This was compounded by the fact that the government appeared to be turning a blind eye to the hole business. When you consider that DC3s were taking off regularly from Villavicencio (a town just 50 miles - 80km from the capital, Bogotá) with cargo doors removed so the fumes from the petrol drums would dissipate, and landing in remote strips where the petrol was used in the production of cocaine, you have to wonder how this could happen in broad daylight with no apparent action being taken. On one Saturday afternoon, we saw five of them take off within a short space of time. Even today, there are still a few DC-3s flying in Colombia, though their numbers are declining.

In 1970, approval had been given for Satena to purchase four new 748 series 2s. These were delivered during 1971. Such were the conditions under which they operated that by mid-1983, three of them had been written off, one of them in extremely bizarre circumstances. The nature of Colombia's mountain ranges, and by extension the frequently-encountered poor weather, together with the use of very old aircraft, many of which were used for drug-running, has given Colombia one of the worst aviation safety records in the world.

The **first** one was actually stolen early one morning from the hangar by a disaffected employee, (he was an engineer, but had learned – unofficially – how to fly the aircraft). He took it up and crashed it on a house in the centre of Bogotá, killing himself and three other people on the ground. Unofficially it is believed that the house was that of his girlfriend whom he believed was having an affair. This must rank as one of the most bizarre aircraft accidents ever recorded.

The **second** one was the only one of the four to leave Colombia in one piece, but was eventually broken up for spares.

Number **three**, came to grief in the Florencia district in the Central Cordillera after hitting a mountain. There are few details about this accident, but people I knew in Satena told me that the two pilots were known for making bets as to how many feet they would clear obstacles by and that this may have been a contributory factor in the accident.

Number **four** ended its flying life at Pasto-Cano airport after landing following a thunderstorm. Fortunately everyone survived the crash, but the aircraft was a write-off.

For a while, Satena used the abandoned DC-3s which they were rescuing from drug-running strips in central Colombia, but they were unreliable and weren't really suitable for some of their routes. Eventually, they decided a further 748 was needed to replace the ones which had crashed. We were contacted by Satena and asked to go over and discuss the purchase of a new aircraft. Visits to Colombia were never without incident, such was the lawlessness in the country at the time. They also wanted a demonstration, and since we had an aircraft in the area at the time, we were able to organise one. On arrival at Bogotá, we needed to clean up the aircraft ready for the demos the following day, a job which included ordering what is euphemistically known in the business as 'the honey cart' to service the toilets.

On arrival at the aircraft, the operative asked where the toilet access valve was and we showed him. However, as he was unwinding the hose from the vehicle, we noticed that the coupling was not compatible with the one on the aircraft. Both myself and my colleague were fluent Spanish speakers and tried to point this out, but the guy was having none of it. "Esto estará bien" (It'll be fine), he said. Well, we knew it wouldn't and we began to walk quickly away from the area. They guy jumped on the back of the truck, opened the cover, forced the coupling into the valve and began to pump.

Airport ramps are noisy places, but we heard his screams above the hubbub and turned around to see the entire contents of the toilet cascading upon his head. We made sure he wasn't injured in any way, left him to sort himself out and carried on with the preparations for the demo flights the following day.

Eventually, we made our way to the hotel and headed straight for the bar and a few cold beers. The bar wasn't busy and we had noticed a guy sitting alone at the bar, who on hearing us speaking English, came over and introduced himself. He was a Louisiana oilman who was working with one of the oil drilling companies. Colombia has oil deposits, but not in significant quantities to make it an oil exporter at that time.

He had been there for a couple of weeks and in the process had had his watch stolen off his wrist whilst walking in the street in Bogotá. This was a very common occurrence at the time, but no-one had warned him and the watch was apparently of considerable sentimental value, his wife having presented it to him on their 25th wedding anniversary.

We advised him to go to Calle Cartoce (14th Street) where it was well-known locally that there were lines of trestle tables on the pavement with vendors selling goods of questionable origin, but to take a local with him to do the negotiating.

We left the following morning for Mitú, a small agricultural town near the border with Brazil, which was deep in the jungle. A company flying agricultural products was based here; they too were operating WWII transport aircraft and were looking for something more modern.

The airport runway consisted of a strip which had been graded from a piece of level land, which was commonly used for grazing by the local horses. In fact as we arrived we spotted several horses on the field, but a gentle low pass soon informed them of our intentions and we were able to land without any further problems.

Within minutes, people began to appear from nowhere. The terminal building was best described as rudimentary and security was non-existent. Clearly this was an exciting event for the locals and it seemed as though the whole town had turned out.

We awaited the arrival of the owner of the cargo company, who duly arrived in an example of his fleet which, even then, was 40 years old. He was wearing what can only be described as a robe and Jesus sandals and these, together with a bushy beard, had us wondering whether we were witnessing a reincarnation.

After the usual pleasantries and discussions, we prepared the aircraft for the demo flight. The crowds were shooed away and the doors closed. Yours truly had elected to stay behind. The was a strict rule that one of us always stayed behind with a passenger list and other details, just in case the worst should happen.

The demo took place, the owner stayed around for a little while after and then wandered over to his own aircraft and took off. We never heard from him or his company again, but a casual conversation back in Bogotá a few days later revealed that whilst it was true that they were moving produce out of the jungle, not all of it was what you would expect to find on the shelves of your local supermarket!

So, we returned to Bogotá and as we arrived at the hotel, we were met by the Louisiana oilman, who was wearing a wide grin and shouting "The drinks are on me!" Apparently a relative of the concierge who spoke English had taken him down to Calle 14 and he had found his watch on one of the vendor's tables, just as we had predicted.

The following day we had another demo, but yours truly was despatched to collect a quantity of water methanol. For many years, water methanol was used as a coolant in various types of aircraft engines, including jet engines, in order to cool the engine's propulsion chamber during the time the engine is required to work under difficult conditions, i.e. take-offs from airfields which have hot ambient temperatures and are situated high above sea level. For example the main airport at Bogotá, which sits at 2,548 m /8,300ft above sea level. The ambient temperature, even at that altitude is typically 22C during the day which is not surprising when you realise that Bogotá is just 4 degrees north of the Equator.

So off we went that morning in an Islander, a small 8-seater, built on the Isle of Wight, but with most of the seats removed to accommodate the container of water-meth on the return journey from the coastal city of Buenaventura (which translates as *Good Luck*), the largest seaport in Colombia and the only place which seemed to have any water-meth available. Our luck was in and we managed to purchase a 50-litre container of the coolant for cash from a chemical plant on the outskirts of the city and to persuade the taxi driver to take us back to the airport, though he was understandably somewhat reluctant at first. There can be few people in the world who have claimed for water-methanol on their travelling expenses and yes, I did get a receipt!

Back to Bogotá in our little 8 seater, avoiding the high mountains and flying down beautiful valleys, because the aircraft was unpressurised and its navigation equipment was somewhat limited. Fortunately, the weather was kind and we arrived back at Bogotá with the important cargo before nightfall.

With the water-meth tanks topped up, we headed off to Cerrejón the following day. At the time, confirmation that coal had been discovered in huge quantities – in an area to the extreme north-east of Colombia near the border with Venezuela – had been announced by the government. Mining operations were to begin as soon as possible, since the coal was open-cast and required relatively little extraction for this type of mineral.

However, as is so often the case with fossil fuels, the source was located in a very remote area and one of the biggest difficulties was going to be moving the mining crews to and from the site. The original operators had decided that this could only be done by air from the local towns of Puerto Bolivar, which at the time was simply a small port, and Santa Marta, a more significant port, both on the Caribbean coast of Colombia. At the time, the 'runway' was simply a piece of ground which had been levelled and graded, but not sealed. There were no radio beacons to guide us to the airfield and no air traffic control at the site.

We checked the weather for the area and all appeared to be well, so off we went. The area was indeed extremely remote, with not even a lone hut apparent in the vicinity. It has been said that the area was the inspiration for Gabriel Garcia Marquez' book *One Hundred Years of Solitude*. The demonstration went ahead without any problems and we returned to Bogotá.

On our return to the UK, we put together the bid response, but because we had been so busy, we suddenly realised that we were fast approaching the cut-off date. The company running the bid was based in San Francisco, and would only accept submissions in person. So close was the cut-off date that one of my colleagues was sent out on Concorde to New York, with an immediate transfer to San Francisco in order to ensure that the bid would be delivered on time – lucky man!

Our competitor for the deal was the Canadian-built DHC Dash 7 and it was the eventual winner, partly because the buyers of the aircraft felt that for such a remote operation, a four-engined aircraft was essential. At the time of writing, the Dash 7s are still operating.

Nowadays, the mine and the scale of operations is enormous. The operational area covers 170,000 acres (69,000 hectares). Each train which leaves the mine carries about 10,000 tonnes of coal the 93 miles (150km) to Puerto Bolivar every trip.

Back in Bogotá, we had several meetings with Satena and another demonstration took place to one of their busier routes at Medellín, which is another high airport at 1,505m / 4,940ft. Because of its location in a valley between two mountains, there were a number of accidents at the airport, and there was a local joke that the cemetery at one end of the runway was conveniently located.

Medellin had the unenviable reputation at the time of being the most violent city in the world. It was the home of the Medellin Cartel, the most powerful drug cartel in the world, led and funded by Pablo Escobar. This particular piece of information was not at the forefront of our minds when, after a day of demonstrations, we were preparing the aircraft for the following day. However, as we looked through the aircraft windows, we saw a convoy of vehicles arriving.

All of them were large people-carriers and all were black. It was obvious who they were. We had not expected any late visitors and, knowing that kidnapping was a daily occurrence at the time, we were very nervous. They had obviously got through the security controls with no problem at all, so they had connections.

They pulled up by the rear door and climbed the steps. We were polite, but very apprehensive. They were polite and inquisitive. How far could it fly? What was the maximum payload? Can a large freight door be fitted? How stable was the aircraft in cruising mode? An unusual question, the significance of which became clear a little later. They asked some more questions and wandered around the cabin, but showed no interest in the flight deck. They asked whether this type of aircraft had ever been used to carry horses, to which we replied that it had.

This explained the large freight door and the stability questions. Horses are notoriously nervous inside aircraft, especially when there's any turbulence around. Were they just typical questions, or was there genuine interest? We were still feeling nervous, but they were polite and asked the name of our agent in Bogotá before leaving.

We never heard any more from them, but the agent did. He received an order for a new helicopter, to be delivered from the US and this was accompanied by a significant deposit. The order was subsequently cancelled but the agent refused to refund the deposit.

One morning a few weeks later, I had a meeting arranged with one of the partners at the agent's office. I was shown into reception and given coffee. Time went by and there was very little activity in the office, which was very unusual. Eventually, one of the other partners came into reception and invited me into his office. He explained that there would be no meetings today. The partner I had arranged the meeting with had been kidnapped the previous evening on his way out of the office. A ransom, which equated exactly to the deposit for the helicopter, had been demanded from the CEO of the agents for his release. Such was his influence, that he was able to go to the bank and extract the money he needed in the middle of the night and arrange the payment. His partner in the agency was quickly released unharmed, but obviously needed a few days to recover. Nothing more was spoken of the incident and the police did not become involved.

The Colombian police had an unenviable task in those days. Some were under the influence of the drug barons, the public were suspicious of them, and because of the widespread lawlessness, they were short of resources.

I only had one brush with the police during all my visits there. One evening, in the coastal town of Barranquilla I had arranged to meet some old friends in a restaurant. I took a taxi from outside the hotel and we headed off towards the restaurant. At one point during the journey, the driver took a wrong turn and then found himself heading towards a police roadblock. On seeing this, he attempted, not very successfully as it transpired, to do a swift u-turn. There were shouts of 'alto!' (stop!) He was reluctant, so I told him to stop immediately and the police ran over. We were taken out of the car and put against a wall.

Fortunately, I had my passport with me and explained that I had hired the taxi to take me to a restaurant in the town, whilst the one of the policemen pointed a useful-looking assault rifle at my vital organs. Meanwhile the driver was being interviewed a short distance away. A few minutes later, I saw him being hand-cuffed and wondered whether I was next. Once he had been put into a police car, the senior officer came over to me and asked which restaurant I was going to. I told him and he promptly arranged for a police car to take me the rest of the way. He also asked which hotel I was staying in. He said he would call at the hotel the following day.

My friends were, to say the least, a little surprised when I turned up at the restaurant in a local police car!

The police officer duly arrived at the hotel the following day. He was principally concerned to know whether I knew the taxi driver, which I didn't. Having established that I didn't, he explained that the reason the road was blocked off was because they were doing a drugs bust and when the taxi started to make a swift exit from the scene, they were sure it was in some way involved. Apparently, the vehicle I had been travelling in was not a licensed taxi, despite the fact that it had a lighted sign on the roof. The driver did not have a licence or insurance. He had apparently bought the taxi sign in a second-hand shop and decided to park outside the hotel in the hope of some business.

Many of the taxis in Colombia were unlicensed, though there was no certain way of knowing those which were and those which weren't. On one occasion I came out of the front door of our hotel to find my colleague, who had gone ahead of me to arrange a taxi, pinned up against the wall by a huge taxi driver. I immediately alerted the concierge, who talked him into releasing him. Apparently the driver had become upset after my colleague refused to get into the taxi because it only had three doors.

Eventually, Satena was able to convince the Colombian government, via the Air Force, to release funds. The usual contract negotiations took place which, all things considered, were relatively easy, helped by the fact that we used the previous contract as a basis for the new one. Thus the contract was signed within a couple of months and an aircraft was allocated for delivery.

It was collected in August 1981 by a crew from Satena, who ensured that the trip to the UK was worthwhile, having filled up any available space with luxury items which attracted heavy taxes in their own country. Colombia levied a high tax on luxury goods (including imported cars) in those days.

The aircraft stayed in Satena service until 1997, when it was bought by a cargo carrier called West Air Europe in Sweden and fitted with a large freight door. It eventually found its way to South Sudan and has the dubious distinction of becoming one of the first aircraft to crash in the newly-declared independent country in February 2014.

The 748 taking off from the airstrip in Mitú, Colombia [author]

The VARIG Samba (1986–88)

Sociedade Anônima Empresa de Viação Aérea Rio Grandense (VARIG) was the first national airline established in Brazil. It was founded in 1927 in Porto Alegre, southern Brazil by Otto Ernst Meyer-Labastille, a German aviator decorated in World War I, who had arrived in Brazil in 1921 and realised how necessary air transportation was for such a large country. In terms of area, Brazil is almost the same size as the USA.

Back in 1986, we had heard that Varig were thinking about replacing their fleet of 15 four-engined turbo-prop Lockheed Electra aircraft on what is known in Brazil as the *Ponte Aérea* (Air Bridge) between the down-town airports of Rio and Sao Paulo. The route was nominally controlled by Varig but they shared the costs and revenue with **Viação Aérea São Paulo S/A** (VASP) who, unusually for an airline, were owned by the state government of São Paulo, and two private companies called Cruzeiro and Transbrasil. The air bridge in its current form began in 1975. It is believed to have been the first ever shuttle operation and the only one of any significance still operating. The combined population of greater Rio and São Paulo is approximately 20 million and whilst there is a luxury bus service between the two cities, it takes between four and five hours and is not particularly cheap. There is no train service, although there has long been talk of high-speed connection. The distance between the two is approximately an hour's flying time.

The Electras first began operating on the route in 1962 and had given good service, but were now becoming unreliable. The operation ran from 0600 to 2300 every day (an average of 66 flights daily) and that there were departures every 15 minutes during most of that time, so aircraft reliability was very important, since most flights were full and any cancellations caused a lot of problems, not least with a build-up of passengers. The frequencies were reduced at weekends.

The service was largely aimed at the business community, though the aircraft were in an all-economy configuration, typically with 85 seats. Since the aircraft had been bought second-hand from several US airlines, the seating configurations varied somewhat. My personal favourites were the ones with the lounge-type seating arrangement at the rear of the aircraft.

The airports at both ends of the Air Bridge are unusual. Rio's down-town airport of Santos Dumont (SDU), named after the French aviator, is an interesting one. The airfield and terminal buildings were constructed in 1936, though not in the art-deco style which was prevalent at the time. The entire interior of the original building was finished in marble, which was rather fortuitous, because in 1999, a fire, allegedly caused by a faulty ATM, broke out in the terminal building. Fires in airport terminal buildings are extremely rare, but this broke out late at night after the building had been closed, and was not immediately apparent. What made matters worse was the fact that when the fire brigade arrived, they discovered the hydrants were short of water, following a recent drought. Water had to be taken from the nearby bay, but although it helped put out the fire, the damage from seawater was an added factor in delaying the return to service of the terminal building, so for six months, passengers travelling on the air bridge had the unique experience of checking in inside an aircraft hangar.

The biggest problem has always been that there is nothing more which can be done to extend the existing runways, because the airfield juts out into Guanabara Bay. At one end of the parallel runways is the famous Sugar-Loaf Mountain, standing at 400 metres high. At the other end is a bridge across the bay with an eight-lane road bridge which rises as it crosses the bay in order to allow ocean-going ships to pass underneath on their way to the nearby docks. In fact, the runways have already been extended to their maximum length, but are totally unsuitable for large passenger aircraft. All long haul flights operate from the main international airport. The longer of the two parallel runways at SDU is just 1,300 metres, or just over 4,300 feet – short by the standards of any major airport. It must be the closest airport to any major business centre in the world. From our agent's office, it was a mere 10-minute walk to the check-in desks. The banking, legal, industrial and insurance organisations all have their headquarters in the city centre. At the other end of the route, Congonhas Airport in São Paulo is equally unique. It was the headquarters of VASP, the airline owned by São Paulo State. The airport also opened in 1936, and at the time of opening was some distance from the centre of the city.

Nowadays it is completely surrounded by multi storey blocks of houses and offices. Like Santos Dumont, it has parallel runways, one a similar length to SDU and the other slightly longer at just under 2,000m / 6,000 feet. For this reason it is known to the Brazilian aviation community as 'the aircraft carrier'. It is further out from the city centre than SDU but still near enough to be attractive to the business community. Indeed, one side of the airport is given over to hangarage for business jets.

From an operational point of view, the Electra was a good match. It was capable of a much longer range of course and had optimum seating, but equally it was, at the time, perfect for the route. Despite being almost 30 years old, the aircraft were generally very reliable and well-maintained, but as with any machinery of that age, the maintenance requirements and thus costs were constantly increasing and reliability was becoming a problem.

Thus began the process of selecting a replacement. Three types were considered, the British Aerospace 146-200, the Boeing 737-300 and the Dutch-built Fokker 100. We all produced studies showing how we felt the flights could continue to operate in a similar style to the current ones, with fuel usage, training and maintenance costs, etc. The F-100 was rejected at an early stage, primarily because it could not operate fully-loaded, even from the longer of the two SDU runways.

Regular discussions took place with Varig to determine how the operation would work and what the seating configuration would be, the galley space, etc. Even on a short trip such as this, Varig provided a full catering service; coffee (of course!) or tea and sandwiches on the morning flights and drinks and snacks on the evening flights, all of which were included in the ticket price.

So finally, it came down to a straight competition between the 737-300 and the BAe 146-200. Varig asked for demonstrations of both aircraft, which caused us a bit of a problem, because we didn't have a 146 operating in South America at the time and none was available in the US. We had already started to plan how we would get the 146 from Hatfield to Rio, which was going to take about six days, given that the 146 was built for neither range nor speed and we were busy working out routes via Greenland and Iceland, when, out of the blue, we discovered that the Queen's Flight (as it was then known) was taking a 146-100 aircraft to Brazil to support a visit by Princess Anne.

Discussions were held with 32 squadron at RAF Benson (where the Queen's Flight was based at the time) to see whether we could 'borrow' it for the demo. Of course it was not representative of a standard 146 but the most important thing was to show how it would cope with the short runway at SDU. A lot of protocol was involved and it eventually came down to "Well, if the Queen is OK with it, then we'll do it." Thankfully, she was, so we set about planning the demo.

The aircraft was being used by Prince Philip on World Wildlife Fund business and his journey was finishing in Belize. Princess Anne was flying down to Rio on British Airways, so it was agreed that I would meet the crew in Belize and we'd take the aircraft down from there, so I could brief them on the way down. The RAF still had a presence there at the time, because the Guatemalans had been causing trouble on the border and down town Belize City had been declared unsafe.

We set off the following morning, stopped in the Brazilian city of Manaus for fuel and lunch and then Brasilia for the overnight stay and a courtesy visit to the embassy. In the meantime, O Globo TV (the Brazilian equivalent of Sky) had heard about the forthcoming demo and wanted to broadcast the 146's arrival live on TV. We had to adjust the timings to fit in with their schedule, but it was well worth it, given the publicity it would attract.

Air Traffic Control for all aircraft in Brazil was handled by the military in those days but the Defence Attaché in Brasilia had good contacts, and we were allowed to fly down Copacabana and Ipanema beaches on the way in. This gave us an opportunity to show how quiet the 146 was in comparison with its competitors. We were able to watch the playback later that evening and the excitement of the Brazilian commentator on our arrival was reminiscent of a Brazil/Argentina football match.

The aircraft was then handed back to Princess Anne for a few days, which gave us a bit of breathing space to set up the demos, which are always complicated affairs. To complicate the issue further, we were told that a kidnap threat had been made against Princess Anne and security would be increased, but there would be no change to her schedule. We were particularly pleased about this, as she had agreed to attend a reception we were holding for the great and good of Varig and Rio the evening after the demo and we were able to ask her to thank her mother for letting us borrow the aircraft. So the day of the demo dawned. Thankfully, the weather was OK, so no problems there, but without giving too much away, there are a limited number of useful seats on the Queen's Flight aircraft, so we had to manage the invites and the seating very carefully. There is never a shortage of passengers for demo flights, but it's obviously important that the right people get to fly on them and come off the aircraft with the right experience. We had also invited the VASP management in São Paulo to join us, so we had the additional headache of how to deal with them. We decided to rent a large room in São Paulo's down-town airport in Congonhas (CGH) and have people available to give presentations, answer questions and generally make themselves useful, so that we could entertain the Rio contingent while the VASP people had their turn of flying down to the *Cidade Marvilhosa* – as the residents of Rio call it.

It's worth mentioning that there is a certain amount of none-too-friendly rivalry between the two cities. São Paulo is viewed as the hard-working hub of industry whereas the *Cariocas* (residents of Rio) are seen as hedonists by the *Paulistanos* (residents of São Paulo). Everyone is familiar with Rio's concrete statue of *Christ the Redeemer* with its outstretched arms. Paulistanos say that it will clap its hands the day someone in Rio does any work – and don't even mention the futebol!

All went well. By now, the Varig chief pilot and myself had built up a good working relationship and he gave me some very useful feedback both on management's thoughts and his own on the aircraft. It was clear that they felt the 146 was a serious competitor, but more studies were needed. VASP were not so easy to convince; they loved their existing Boeing 737-200s, although these could not be used on the air bridge and had ordered the larger 737-300 for their other services. The other two were prepared, in general, to go along with Varig. So the demonstrations were completed and we went away and did some more sums. We looked again at the interior arrangements, galley, seating, bulkheads etc, all of which had to be done within strict weight limits, and came up with costings. The engineering boys came up with a support package and the pilots with crew training.

We took the whole proposal back a few weeks later, talked them through it and left them to think about it. About three weeks later we were called back again for further discussions. We were told (very unofficially) that we were the preferred bidder. One of the reasons for this was because they had written a programme of their own and run it through their Boeing 737-300 rudimentary simulator and found that under certain weather conditions, i.e. heavy rain, the 737-300 could not land at SDU. They contacted Boeing, who initially denied their claims, but Varig took their program to Boeing's headquarters in Seattle and ran it on their simulator, and proved their point. Boeing now had a problem. A fix could be done, but it would cost time and money, neither of which Varig had budgeted for. A few more weeks passed and we were called back again.

By this time, Boeing had claimed that they would fix the problem, but not immediately and there would be a cost, but gave no details of either. On this basis, Varig would be paying significantly more per aircraft for the 737-300 than they would for the 146 and we moved into pole position. A meeting of all the companies involved in the Air Bridge took place and it was agreed that the 146 would be the winning bid. However, the information soon reached the ears of Boeing's agent in Brazil and a frantic round of diplomatic activity began. There was no way that Boeing wanted to lose a deal like this, but they were really up against it with little room for manoeuvre from a performance point of view, and they knew it. Senior politicians from Washington, accompanied by equally senior beings from Boeing began to arrive and the Brazilian government was put under a lot of pressure, despite the fact that Varig was actually a private company.

Fast forward several weeks and I was in Paraguay when I received a message to call in to Rio on the way home. I went to the agent's office and they said that the chief pilot wanted to talk to me, but would not explain why. I called him and we agreed to meet for lunch. I could tell from the moment he walked into the restaurant that it was not good news, because he wasn't his normal cheerful self. We sat down at the table and he said *"vamos falar em Português"* (let's speak Portuguese) because he knew I spoke it and he said it was easier for him to explain in his own language. He began first to explain his (and the company's) embarrassment and disagreement with the decision, which had gone the way of Boeing. He said that the US government had put a huge amount of pressure on the Brazilian government to buy the Boeings. Basically, this revolved around a recent trade mission from the US, which was about to buy a large amount of Brazilian products: fruit, juices, shoes, steel and other items. These purchases would be cancelled if the decision went against Boeing. The government, seeing the potential problems of the loss of dollar sales, and with inflation rampant at the time, had to capitulate. (Inflation rates were such that people were being employed to go into supermarkets at night to mark up the prices from the previous day.)

So that was it. A potential 350 million dollar deal and 18 months of work had gone down the toilet because of politics and there was nothing anyone could do about it. It was a very sad person who checked in for the Varig flight back to London that night. I was upgraded to First Class with no-one sitting next to me – the ultimate upgrade (the remainder of F was full) – and I know who did that and why. Fortunately Varig had very good food and especially drinks on their flights and I made good use of both during the 12-hour flight back home.

We received a formal letter from Varig confirming their decision about 10 days later. There were times when I hated the job!

Two years later I was in Brazil on other business and met their chief pilot again. He told me that the promised modifications to allow the 737-300 to land at SDU in bad weather had not materialised, so whenever it rained heavily there, they had to divert to Rio's main international airport. I was not surprised.

Breathless in Bolivia (1986)

I never really understood why we hadn't sold the 748 to Bolivia. After all, it ticked all the boxes for operations there; the ability to land on short and/or unprepared runways, a much better 'hot and high' capability than its competitors, and the provision of a large freight door if it was required, which the current turbo-props operating there did not have. Here I should perhaps explain the meaning of hot and high. Aircraft engines are designed to operate in extremely cold air, since that is where they spend most of their time. They don't like having to work at hot temperatures and high altitude while they're still on the ground, because it significantly reduces their power output. An example of this is a summer flight from Johannesburg (airport altitude 1700m/5500 feet) to London with a full load of fuel and passengers. There were many occasions when the flight would be delayed until the temperature had dropped a few degrees in order to ensure the engines were able to cope with the task ahead of them.

We had demonstrated the 748 to Bolivia a couple of times, but the national carrier Lloyd Aero Boliviano, (LAB) had never shown much interest. We knew they had something of a fixation about propeller–driven aircraft despite the fact that they had several different types of turboprops, which, apart from anything else, complicated the engineering planning. They may have had a point, because Bolivia is a very mountainous country and has the world's highest international airport at La Paz. The airport is actually 1000 feet higher than the city itself, but more of this later.

The use of 'Lloyd' as the prefix to the airline's name, had always intrigued me, because it is not the sort of family name you expect to find in Bolivia. Apparently it had been chosen because they knew of Lloyd's of London and their reputation for security and safety and had thus incorporated it into the airline's name. It seems to have had little effect however, because their accident record is one of the worst I have ever seen for what was a relatively small airline.

There are two other major cities in Bolivia; Cochabamba and Santa Cruz. Of these, Santa Cruz, at a mere 1,370 feet above sea level, is the lowest, and had been chosen the engineering base. Being the capital, La Paz might seem the more obvious choice, but calibrating sophisticated aircraft engines at 11,000 feet is not to be recommended. Because of this, Santa Cruz was actually the principal hub, because the few international airlines which operated into Bolivia at the time preferred to operate from an airport at a lower altitude. Bizarrely, the headquarters of the airline were not at the capital, or the maintenance base, but at a third city, Cochabamba.

Santa Cruz had a claim to fame. The story goes that in 1971, a Lockheed Constellation had made a refuelling stop at the airport while on a flight from Miami to Montevideo and then took off again without authorisation. The local authorities became suspicious and it was chased by two World War II era fighters, one of whose pilots was killed when his aircraft crashed during the chase. The Constellation was forced to land, the crew were arrested and when the aircraft was inspected later they found smuggled goods (whisky and cigarettes) on board. It may seem strange to be smuggling cigarettes and whisky over such a long distance, but in those days there were very heavy duties levied on imports of all kinds into Uruguay. Cars, for example, were taxed at 200% and for many years it rivalled Cuba for its collection of old cars. The aircraft was fenced off where it came to rest on military territory and stayed there for many years, principally because the means to move it was not available and the military wanted it left there as a reminder to others. As the years passed, people began to build houses in the area, so there it sat, with bushes and houses growing around it, in the middle of what eventually became a housing estate. It has now been moved closer to the centre of the city in a children's park and is now labelled as *El Avion Pirata* (no translation required!).

However, a lot of our time was spent at El Alto (the high one) airport at La Paz. The city itself is at 12,000 feet above sea level, but the airport sits on a plateau at just over 13,000 feet. I don't know how many airports were equipped with full medical facilities in those days, but El Alto was. Many was the time we would see a medical team rush out to an inbound aircraft with an oxygen cylinder and a wheelchair. Having witnessed this many times, we were almost in need of it ourselves one evening when we returned to the hotel to discover that the lifts weren't working – and we were on the fifth floor!

Because of the poor road network at that time, meat from the fertile plains in the interior of the country was flown into La Paz by whatever aircraft was available, principally with old WWII transport aircraft. There were many crashed and abandoned aircraft outside the airport perimeter, and many more in flying condition within the airfield itself. There was no refrigeration at any point during the journey other than possibly some chilling during the flight and it was said that the time between slaughter and arrival in the markets of La Paz was no more than five hours.

About a year before our visit, Short Brothers had taken a small 30-seater turboprop, designated 330, on a demo tour to Bolivia. The aircraft had sold successfully around the world, even to the US Air Force. However, someone back in Sydenham (Short Brother's factory at what is now known as George Best International Airport) obviously hadn't done their sums properly, because after no less than eight attempts to get airborne from El Alto, the aircraft had to be dismantled and taken out in a cargo aircraft!

Even in a less than full Braniff Airlines DC-8 heading for Dallas, the take-offs were always interesting and the captain would warn everyone of the likelihood of the aircraft "dropping a little after take-off".

On one occasion we were doing the 25-minute flight down to Cochabamba on an LAB Boeing 727 when, just after take-off, the oxygen masks deployed without any warning. There was no panic in the cabin, so we suspected that it was not such an unusual occurrence and put it down to finger-trouble on the flight deck because the aircraft had failed to pressurise after take-off, and we returned to the airport. About 20 minutes later the aircraft was ready for take-off again with the oxygen masks re-stowed. At least we hoped they were! My engineering colleague wondered whether they had actually re-stowed them or just cut them off because he reckoned it had been done in record time. He did concede though that the efficiency was perhaps because it was a regular occurrence!

On another occasion, I was asked to go to Potosi, which had once been the centre of the silver mining industry. The airport had been closed for more than a year and the roads in the surrounding area were rudimentary, to say the least. The airport stood at more than 12,000 feet, and they had been looking at the possibility of using the 19-seat Jetstream 31 for their routes, which would be mostly internal.

Now the J31 is a bit of what is known in aviation circles as a "ground-hugger", which basically means that its take-off performance is not too sparkling. Fearing a repeat of the Short 330 débâcle, we suggested the 748 might be a better option. This required much discussion but for some reason the thin air began to affect me more than it had previously. We abandoned the discussions and hastened to the hotel, which was at a slightly lower altitude, where I was a given a cup of green tea with a coca leaf floating on the top. This apparently is a standard and legal remedy for *Gringos* suffering from *sorochi* or 'mountain sickness'. Anyway, it worked and the following day we were able to conclude the discussions.

However, the price of Bolivia's biggest natural resource at the time, tin, was falling rapidly on world markets; it transpired that the local silver mines had been all but exhausted at the time, and the economy was in a bad way, so there was no follow-up.

I did not go back to Bolivia again, there were too many other interesting prospects to follow up. And if I were to go there today, I suspect I would be one of those requiring the oxygen cylinder and wheelchair at El Alto!

One of the two tyres which burst on landing at Quito. Tyre-changing at 9000 feet is not to be recommended! [Author]

Cuban Capers (1986)

Probably the best-known airline in Cuba is **Cubana** but in the early 80s another Cuban-based airline appeared on the scene. **Aero Caribbean** was originally established in 1982 as **Empresa Aero**. It was set up by the Cuban government to provide domestic services and occasional charters to supplement the national carrier, Cubana. It was of course wholly owned by the government of Cuba, as was everything else at the time. Its fleet (such as it was) consisted of two Bristol Britannias, built in 1960 and a number of Soviet Antonov 24s and 26s, similar in size and looks to the F-27, which was so often our competitor. Nominally, they were used for domestic routes but, prior to the invasion of Grenada, they were flying into Pearls airport on a regular basis until one was captured there during the invasion by the US invasion in 1983, following the love-in between Michael Manley (Grenada's President) and Fidel Castro, which eventually brought about the invasion of Grenada referred to elsewhere in this book.

Cubana's maintenance abilities were rather limited, however maintenance would not be a problem in this case, since there were numerous 748 operators in the Caribbean at the time and it would have been easy to fly the aircraft to another 748 operator in the area. The Britannias were a different story; they had to be flown to Monarch Airlines at Luton for major maintenance, since at the time they were the only other operator of the type. They ended their lives with Aero Caribbean flying freight to and from Canada, before being withdrawn from use in 1987.

Soviet aircraft in those days were notoriously unreliable and support was badly lacking. Despite having good relations with the

Soviet Union, Cuba could not persuade them to supply sufficient spares and the aircraft spent most of their time on the ground, which led them to approach us. Of course there were many restrictions on selling anything into Cuba at the time, particularly if it had US content. However, just like the Britannia, the 748 could be delivered with entirely British components on board and, provided we could obtain an export certificate from the UK Board of Trade, which we were assured we could, there would be no problem in supplying such an aircraft.

Cuba was not an easy place to reach in those days and the only practical way to fly there was via Mexico City with **Mexicana**, the state airline. Check-in for flights to Cuba would be in a separate area of the terminal, visas would be checked there and once again at the boarding gate. There would be few announcements and it was almost as though the flight didn't exist.

Once, there, I checked into the Hotel Havana Riviera on the seafront. The hotel had formerly been the jewel in the crown of hotels in Cuba but was now looking a little the worse for wear. No floor dragons and, surprisingly perhaps for this part of the world, I did not see any cockroaches during my stay.

I had several meetings with Aero Caribbean to determine how they would use the aircraft. There was none of the formality I had experienced in meetings in the Soviet Union in a previous occupation. No KGB character taking notes, or the hushed tension when the head of the department arrived at a T-shaped table in a large office. They were friendly and at times jovial – just the sort of thing I had experienced elsewhere in the Caribbean.

They gave me a brief on the background of the company and explained that since the main island of Cuba is such a large island at 1,250km (780 miles) long and there was little in the way of transport infrastructure at the time. The journey time by road between Havana and Santiago de Cuba, the country's second city, would typically take about 12 hours. Even a flight between the two cities by 748 would take the better part of two hours. We examined possible domestic routings and flights to Jamaica and Guyana. At the time, Guyana was nominally a democracy, but the President, Forbes Burnham, had strong Socialist views and was very much a fellow-traveller of the Cuban government. Guyana Airways also operated the 748 and would probably have been first choice for maintenance.

Clearly regular air services within Cuba and to its smaller out-lying islands would have to be subsidised by the government and they were prepared to do this. We ran lots of numbers and left with them proposals for both new and used aircraft. Unfortunately, shortly afterwards, the economy began to collapse, largely because of a depressed world sugar market and a prolonged drought. As if this was not enough, a fall in the value of the dollar brought the final blow, and the export of foreign currency was severely curtailed, which meant that only what the government deemed as essential foreign purchases were allowed.

Since then, of course, tourism has become a major industry in Cuba and Aero Caribbean has gone from strength to strength, providing much-needed domestic routes in and around Cuba and to other Caribbean islands. These services are now provided by the French-built ATR series of aircraft.

Paraguayan Peregrinations (1986-87)

One of our principal sales targets at BAe was of course the venerable DC-3, since the 748 had been designed as a DC-3 replacement. In South America in the 1980s, DC-3s were still being used extensively on domestic flights both by civil airlines and the military. There were few air forces who didn't have some DC-3s in their fleet, and Paraguay was no exception.

One of the poorest countries in South America, largely because unlike its neighbours, Paraguay has few natural resources, its major industry was clothing production, which was then bought by Argentinians and Brazilians at much lower prices than were available in their own countries. The remainder of the economy revolved largely around agriculture.

During a visit there, we were having a discussion with the head of LAP, the national airline. He mentioned that the Air Force DC-3s were becoming unreliable and spares were becoming increasingly difficult to find. He suggested I contact the Air Force to see if they would be interested in talking to us.

I went to the Embassy, who made some enquiries and told me that first I would have to meet the President (Stroessner) in order to make an approach to the Air Force. Of course, you can't just call his office and ask if you can pop round tomorrow, though Stroessner was famous for rarely leaving the country. He wasn't a popular leader and he knew it, and he felt that there was always the opportunity for a coup if he went abroad.

A meeting was arranged, and I turned up in my best suit at 1100 on the appointed day. Stroessner was famous for keeping people waiting – his German roots had long ago morphed into Latin-

American timekeeping habits. While I waited in the palace foyer a shoe-shine guy came in so I gave him some business and watched the comings and goings, including a stray dog which wandered in, sniffed around, cocked its leg on a table and walked out. It was obviously a regular occurrence because no-one turned a hair. Mind you, having followed a guy carrying four large catfish on his back down a nearby street on my way to the palace, nothing surprised me any more!

Eventually I was ushered in to see the leader. He was polite, but appeared rather uninterested. This opinion was reinforced by a constant procession of staff asking him to sign papers. He asked which hotel I was staying in and said someone would be in touch. Later that day, when I returned to the hotel, there was a message to call a Colonel Duarte, which I did. He said I should be at the airport the following morning at 7am, because we were going to do some flying!

So next morning there I was at the FAP (Paraguayan Air Force) Transport Unit at Aeropuerto Presidente Stroessner (!) where I reported to Col Duarte, who briefed me on what we were going to do. It seemed that we were going on a whistle-stop tour of Paraguay in a 40-year old military DC-3 to deliver supplies to both military and civil townships throughout Paraguay. There were some rudimentary seats on board, with ample room for freight and the aircraft had a large freight door. Initially, I sat in the unconverted radio operator's position, just behind the cockpit, equipped only with a 'letterbox' window, which meant that initially I could enjoy very little of the passing scenery. However, once we were at cruising height, the co-pilot (who turned out to be Stroessner's son) wandered off to chat to the hostess (also in military uniform) and I was invited to take the right-hand seat.

It was a fascinating flight. Since Paraguay is relatively flat, we flew at about 1500 feet between airfields, which allowed a great view of the countryside, including several lakes, where our low-flying disturbed the local flamingo population. At one point, we apparently flew over the house in which Josef Mengele had lived during his stay in Paraguay. We visited five different airfields, three of which had grass strips for runways, at one point carrying a tethered goat between two sectors.

Following the visit, we produced a full report on how we thought the 748 could perform on their routes and returned with it some weeks later. It was a long way to take a 748 for a demo flight, so we agreed with the Brazilian Air Force to borrow one of theirs. I wasn't there for that exercise, but it apparently went well, so we put together a finance package and returned once again.

It became clear at this point that *El Presidente* himself was going to get involved in the decision-making process and we were once again ushered into his room in the palace. We made our pitch, left, and heard nothing more for several weeks, until we got a message from the British Embassy in Asunción saying they had learnt that the Air Force had decided to purchase the Spanish CASA 212.

We were somewhat perplexed by this, since to the best of our knowledge, it had not been one of the aircraft under consideration. Not only that, but it was significantly smaller and unpressurised. Later, discreet enquiries revealed that Stroessner's son-in-law had become the local agent for CASA, though the deal for him to become the agent had only been signed about 10 days before the announcement!

In 1989, Stroessner was deposed after 35 years in power. He went into exile in Brazil, where he lived for another 17 years, dying at the age of 93. Soon after his exile, Asunción airport was re-named Silvio Pettirossi, after a famous Paraguayan aviator.

The Ryanair Revelation (1986)

There can be few people in Europe who have never heard of Ryanair. However, fewer people may be aware of the real beginnings of Ryanair and how what began as a cheaper alternative for Irish ex-pats to get home, turned into the airline we know today.

I knew of Tony Ryan, who at the time was founder and CEO of Guinness Peat Aviation (GPA) – in their day the largest aircraft leasing company in the world – but had never met him, so I was somewhat surprised when my boss asked me to, "Nip over to Shannon and have a chat with Tony Ryan – he's thinking of starting an airline."

"*The* Tony Ryan – and he's looking for 748s?" I asked, knowing that the list of aircraft on their books included almost every type of modern jet airliner operating at the time.

"Apparently so," he answered, "but go over and listen to what he has to say."

I hadn't been to Shannon for many years but when I arrived I discovered that it hadn't changed very much, except for the shiny new building near the airport, which was the GPA headquarters. At the meeting it quickly became clear that Tony Ryan was indeed thinking of setting up an airline. However, instead of us giving a presentation to him, he gave a presentation to us, outlining his vision of becoming a serious competitor to Aer Lingus. Since he had previously worked for Aer Lingus he had the inside track and one of his pet hates was the fact that Aer Lingus fares across the Irish Sea were so high, principally because there was so little competition. British Airways had a very limited operation into all of the Republic's airports at the time and Tony Ryan felt that there was a lot of potential traffic available, none of which was prepared to pay the high fares being asked by the national carrier.

"It's the welly traffic we're after," said Tony Ryan.

"The welly traffic?" I asked. He laughed.

"Yeah, the guys who work on the building sites all over London and want to go home to visit friends and relations. Many of them live in north London, Kilburn mainly, and our plan is to put on a bus service to Luton and operate a flight from there."

The only alternative to flying in those days for Irish people living in the south of England was to take a train from London to Holyhead in Anglesey and then the ferry to Dun Laoghaire, a ferry port south of Dublin – a nine-hour journey at best and always subject to the winds on the Irish Sea. The other alternative for those from the southern counties of the Republic was the train to Fishguard in Wales and then the ferry to Rosslare in south-east Ireland. The journey time was similar.

The Ryanair concept was an interesting one and one which I knew had worked before. During the same era, I had visited a company called ARCO who operated a service across the River Plate between a town called Colonia in Uruguay and Buenos Aires with a couple of American Convair 600s, together with a coach service from Montevideo to Colonia, in order to offer some competition to the Aerolineas Argentinas monopoly between Montevideo and Buenos Aires. The route was eventually abandoned after the see-saw economies of the two countries reduced the traffic considerably.

Following the meeting, we got down to organising a lease for two 748s with a six-month breakpoint. Of course, the whole idea was little more than an experiment and there was no guarantee that the 'welly traffic' would turn up. The aircraft were not new but used ones which had been returned from Dan-Air, but were in good condition and ideal for the job in mind. We took the contract back to Shannon and left it with them for 24 hours to study. The following day, we met Tony Ryan and, together with his two sons, Cathal and Declan, we went through it in detail. A few items needed to be ironed out and we agreed to meet at breakfast next morning to sort them out. Over breakfast we exchanged the usual pleasantries and I asked Tony if he had slept well.

"Slept like a baby."

"That's good."

"No, I woke up screaming every two hours!"

Fortunately he was joking, but there was no more levity. There was so much going on at GPA that his time was very limited, so we quickly finalised the details and the contract was signed.

Surprisingly perhaps, one of the most important items discussed during contract negotiations is the colour scheme for the aircraft, because airlines often use the introduction of new aircraft to present a new colour scheme and sometimes a whole new image. Tony Ryan was keen to launch the airline as quickly as possible and our focus was on preparing the aircraft for service as soon as the contract was confirmed and it was only when the paint shop called and asked what colour scheme to put on the aircraft that we realised it hadn't come up in the discussions. We called them and asked if they had a scheme in mind.

"We hadn't really thought much about that – usually we're told what colour scheme to put on the aircraft," was the reply. Possible schemes were mocked-up and sent over for approval. Finally they decided upon a basic white scheme with a stylised Ryanair logo and a series of lines below window level, all of which looked very smart. The two aircraft were painted up and delivered. They were quickly put into service on the Luton-Dublin route in late 1986 and the rest, as they say, is history.

Certainly Tony Ryan had plans to 'grow' the airline but whether he imagined it would develop to the extent it has is anyone's guess, although by the time he died in 2007 the airline was already well established. Sadly, his eldest son Cathal died just a few months after him. I have to say that he and his family were some of the nicest people I ever met in the airline business. They were keen businessmen but always very pleasant to deal with, often with a sense of humour just below the surface and despite his wealth (Tony Ryan was a euro billionaire when he died), extremely approachable.

Following his death, the airline which carries his name began to take a different turn and became the business as we know it today.

The 748 demonstrator in house colours. [Author]

The SATA Saga (1986-87)

Two and a half hours by jet to the west of Lisbon lie a group of nine islands known as the Azores. They are owned by Portugal and despite the fact that they lie in the middle of the Atlantic, have a benign climate. There is only a 350-mile difference in the distance between the Azores and Newfoundland and the Portuguese mainland. Each island has an airport, though some are better equipped than others. Lajes, which is shared with the US Air Force, is well-known, as is Santa Maria. Ponta Delgada, (PDL) the capital, has a runway capable of handling wide-bodied aircraft, though its runway is shorter than the other two and thereby hangs the tale.

The SATA saga really falls into two distinct parts. **SATA** was the airline which had kept the group of islands together since the early 1970s, most recently with a fleet of three 748s. At that time, they were not allowed to fly outside the Azores, even to Lisbon, so their concentration was entirely on the island group. The 748s had given sterling service since 1977, but these were the older 2A series and the constant take-offs and landings between short hops, coupled with the salt-laden sea air prevalent in island flying, had taken their toll.

We now had a newer version of the aircraft, with improved fuel consumption and better operational performance, which was very useful for the smaller airfields. To ensure that no claims of impropriety could be brought concerning the selection process, SATA also considered the usual competitors, i.e., F-27, Dash 8, and the ATR-42. So the discussions began.

The F-27 was once again eliminated early on, not least because SATA was not entirely sure that a high-winged aircraft was the right choice for a group of islands which were subject to strong winds. As this was 1986, the Dash 8 was still quite new at the time and again unproven for such an operation, which left the ATR-42 as the only other serious competitor.

The basis of the deal was that we would take two of the older series 2A 748s in part-exchange. We did some estimates on the potential resale value of the 748s. They were in good condition, well-maintained, and had a useful amount of well-catalogued spares – or so I thought!

Many people will be familiar with the green-lined computer paper with the holes in the side which existed in the early days of computers. I was given a box full of these, which in effect was a computer print-out of their entire spares holding. I spent the evening going through the list and I noticed the word 'mono' appeared frequently in the lists, but it had a part number against it, which was rather confusing, because one of the meanings of mono in Portuguese is monkey. At the meeting next morning, we brought up the subject with the Chief Engineer. There was much shuffling of feet and embarrassed looks and the CEO said to the Chief Engineer in Portuguese, "You'd better confess – he speaks Portuguese!" It transpired that the items were screws, nuts, bolts and other fastening material on which they'd put a higher value than was realistic. Nice try! A compromise figure was eventually agreed, not without some humour it should be said.

We then got down to the nitty gritty of the trade-in values and a price for the whole package. Basically it's very similar to trading in your old car for a new model. You agree a price for the old one (and the spares) and a price for the new one and set up the financing to cover the difference. We got the numbers to work to the satisfaction of all concerned and drew up a draft contract. The usual negotiations took place, the pencils were sharpened and a deal was agreed.

We went back to Woodford, drew up the contract and returned. Two days were spent going through the new contract and finally everything was agreed. The contract was to be signed the following morning, following which SATA would be holding a press conference. The team went out for dinner, had a drink or two and returned to the hotel.

For some reason, I hadn't really enjoyed the evening and thus hadn't drunk very much. At about 2330, the phone rang in my room. It was the CEO of SATA, who said, "I've just had some disturbing news which I need to discuss with you urgently. I'm sending my car round for you now."

I was taken to his house and shown a fax which referred to the accident of a 748 belonging to Air Illinois in November 1983. I was aware of the situation, but not in detail. The report (which had clearly been doctored) blamed the aircraft for having a poor electrical system, which had been the cause of the accident. Well, it was true that an electrical system had been at fault, but it was equally clear that the National Transportation Safety Board had determined that the cause was pilot error. It was also clear that, having come this far, SATA were not about to change their minds, but they knew that the question would be brought up at the press conference the following morning, because Aerospatiale had a 'plant' amongst the reporters. It later transpired that, unknown to us, an Aerospatiale team were still on the island ready to pounce if SATA had changed their minds, which was obviously part of their cunning plan!

My boss was in Washington, fortunately just three hours behind in time zones and with the help of my Filofax – the 1980s version of an iPad – I managed to find him in a restaurant over there which we used a lot. He agreed to go to the office, dig out the report and fax it over. The signing was postponed for 24 hours while we all got some sleep and waited for a copy of the NTSB accident report to arrive by fax. The next morning the faxes arrived and we had another meeting with the CEO, who said he was satisfied that the aircraft was not at fault and the signing went ahead the following day – phew!

All was well and we climbed aboard the late-night flight back to Lisbon, where, despite it being well after midnight, the agent was waiting to take us out for a celebratory meal. Back at Woodford, two aircraft off the production line were allocated. Somewhat ironically (I always thought) one of them was allocated the registration CS-TAP!

It is now 1988 and SATA are interested in the ATP and the 146. They had been negotiating with the Portuguese government to be allowed to fly to the mainland and were keen to increase tourism to the islands.

At this point it should be mentioned that relations between the Azores and mainland Portugal were less than amicable, not helped by the fact that the daily (and only) connecting flight from Lisbon used to arrive in Ponta Delgada at 2000 hours – too late, of course, for any useful connections to other islands, and requiring anyone who lived outside the capital to find somewhere to stay for the night, because many of the airfields were daylight-only operations. Thus the return flight left at 2100 hours which meant that it arrived in Lisbon at 0030 (the Azores are an hour behind Portugal because of their more westerly location), which was equally useless at the Lisbon end.

The route planning department in TAP were clearly determined to get the rest of the day's more lucrative schedules out of the way before they had to do the government-subsidised route to the Azores!

The choice of aircraft was interesting, too. During that time, we flew on Boeing 707s 727s and 737s, presumably depending on whatever type was available at departure time. However, when TAP had one of their not-infrequent strikes, the Air Force had to drag out a WWII era DC-6 to do the route!

We returned to the Azores several years later to present the ATP to SATA. They felt that the ATP was the most suitable aircraft for

The 146 at Ponta Delgada Azores on demonstration to SATA. [Author]

the job of increasing seat capacity on the domestic routes, but in order to keep the competition level as high as possible, the competitive ATR 72 was kept in the equation.

Trips to the Azores were somewhat unusual, in that we'd spend the morning in the office, head down to Heathrow for the mid-afternoon flight to Lisbon, meet the agent, and then take the evening flight to the capital, Ponta Delgada (PDL). Meetings were strictly on a 5-day-week basis, so we were usually back home at the weekends, which made a pleasant change, though myself and one of the contracts team did have to spend a weekend there, and spent our time driving around looking at shipwrecks, of which there were many. Unfortunately it wasn't the whale-watching season, though we did sometimes see dolphins swimming in the bay at Ponta Delgada.

This time there was none of the drama of the 748 deal, although Aerospatiale kept trying hard with our major competitor, the ATR72. The whole thing was done in a couple of trips, with the 748s we had sold a few years previously being taken in part-exchange. No dramas with spares either this time – they'd learnt their lesson!

We also took a 146 to demonstrate. The aircraft had previously been leased to Pacific Southwest Airlines (complete with the smile on the nose), primarily because it seemed at the time to be a good choice for the PDL-LIS route and also some of the busier internal routes during the summer. However, SATA had plans for direct routes into Europe, now that Portugal had become a member of the EEC (as it then was) and could no longer prevent the Azores from having their own international airline. However, the 146 didn't have the range to reach all the cities in Europe which they wanted to serve, so the matter was not taken any further.

I enjoyed working with what were a very professional team at SATA and I'm pleased to see that they have now become a full international airline in their own right, with a wide network and despite the lack of beaches (which was what we were looking for when we found the shipwrecks), the Azores has become a significant tourist destination in its own right, allowing SATA to go from strength to strength.

British Midland Buys More (1987-88)

I n the mid-1980s, British Midland had the second highest number of 'slots' at Heathrow after British Airways. Slots are basically allocations issued by air traffic control (ATC) to allow landings and take-offs to be controlled, so that the ATC system does not become congested.

For example, a delay in Tenerife may be incurred because inclement weather is expected at the destination in Manchester, five hours later, even though the weather in Tenerife may be fine and traffic is operating normally there. Therefore, the delay is not the fault of the airport of departure. Any delay may be caused by the limitations of airspace between the two airports, or somewhere en-route, where there is a bottleneck. There are numerous such points over Central Europe and France.

In practice, the system is far more complicated than this and because of the complex calculations required, is totally computer-controlled. The slots for all airports in Europe are handled by a unit in Brussels. The slots themselves are extremely valuable, both in financial and operational terms, particularly at Heathrow, where there are more potential movements than there are slots available. Thus, if an airline wants to begin operations into Heathrow, it must first apply for a slot. Assuming there is one available and this is unlikely, they would have to take the slot allocated, which may not be at a time convenient for their operation. The alternative is to buy or trade one from another operator.

Having 13% of the slots at Heathrow put British Midland (BM) in a very strong position at that time, both operationally and financially. It was with this background that BM began to take an interest in the ATP in late 1986.

They had a significant domestic and international network based on Heathrow, although the head office was in Donington Hall, a magnificent stately home near Derby which BM had bought and converted some years earlier. They had a fleet of four-engined Viscount aircraft which had 60 seats in a typical configuration, but they were nearing the end of their useful lives. We were looking for a launch customer for the Advanced Turbo-prop (ATP), so we went over to Donington Hall one day to make a presentation. Our ideas were well received and initial discussions began.

At the time, there were three elements to the domestic operation. British Midland itself, with their aircraft based at Heathrow, Manx Airlines based at Ronaldsway on the Isle of Man and Loganair, based in Glasgow. The Viscounts were operated by British Midland and Manx. Loganair's operation was slightly different, since it served many of the smaller airports in Scotland as well as routes to Northern Ireland and Manchester. Following some detailed route studies and an in-depth investigation into how the ATP might fit into the fleet, a plan began to emerge.

Of course, the competitors were knocking at the doors of Donington Hall as well, so we were kept on our toes during all the negotiations.

What became apparent was that the ATP would be distributed amongst all three companies. Inevitably, however, there was a snag. British Midland had operated a large fleet of Viscounts, some of which were now being withdrawn from service and in fact four of these were sitting in a hangar in what was then known as Teesside airport, the former RAF station at Middleton St George, now known as Durham Tees Valley. BM were anxious to get these off the books, not least because they were paying hangarage fees and ongoing maintenance costs and proposed that we take them in part-exchange as a condition of sale.

This caused some teeth-sucking in the management offices at Woodford. We had never been asked to do this before and frankly we had no idea of their worth in order to be able to fit them into our calculations.

I and one of the contracts team went up to Teesside to take a look at both them and their paperwork. The aircraft were almost 30 years old by this time and had been bought second-hand from South African Airways. They were in good condition but, given their age, there would be little interest in them from the second-hand market, even in less-developed countries, so we were, in effect, looking at scrap value – a whole new experience!

Invariably in business, there is a compromise position, and we eventually reached it when the contracts team agreed a price with a company specialising in scrapping aircraft. The aircraft were immediately stripped of their engines and any other useful equipment. Aircraft engines, even old ones, carry a high scrap value whether they are usable or not and are always the first things to be removed from aircraft which are being taken out of service. It so happens that there is an International Fire Training Centre at Teesside and one of the fuselages ended its life there. I believe it is still being used.

So it was back to Donington Hall to work out some more numbers. We wanted BM as a launch customer and there was clearly a deal to be done. They were British and had a good reputation at the time. (This was prior to the Kegworth accident in 1989.)

An order for 10 ATPs had also been placed by Wings West Airlines, based in San Luis Obispo California, operating as American Eagle Airlines, a feeder airline to the huge American Airlines. However, the allocation was never taken up and British Airways were now showing interest in the ATP, though not as a launch customer and we were keen to find homes for the aircraft which had been allocated to Wings West, lest they become 'white tails', industry jargon for new aircraft which have been built but not sold, since after production the tails have usually been painted white to await the logo of the purchasing operator rather than going to the paint shop immediately after completion.

We had by now received a letter of intent from BM and the next step was to put together a draft contract for submission. A team had been put together and the usual finance, insurance, maintenance, training and support programmes were gone through with a fine tooth comb. At Donington Hall, we read through the contract and made some last minute amendments. However, we were still a bit apprehensive about the whole business. It was, after all a deal for a launch aircraft with a launch customer; we had never done one before and it was unlikely we would ever do it again.

A date and time was fixed for our final submissions at Donington Hall, but we decided to set off early and stop off at a Little Chef en route in order to go through everything once again. So over a set of full English breakfasts, we went through everything once more, being careful not to spill tea over any of the paperwork. The meeting took place and eventually we reached an agreement on pricing and delivery. It just remained for the deal to be run by the BM board and the contract would be signed. This duly took place, and a few days later we went over to collect the signed documents.

Dealing with an operator who was based just 60 miles by road from the factory made a pleasant change from the usual long-haul flying; the only flights we did were to the Isle of Man for discussions on the Manx Airlines aspects of the deal.

Inevitably, because of the number of people involved in such complex negotiations, a buzz quickly went around the factory, but we were anxious to keep the deal under wraps, because both we and BM wanted to announce the deal officially at the 1987 Paris Air Show, where it would obtain maximum publicity, but this was a few months away, so everyone was sworn to secrecy.

Five aircraft would be delivered initially; BM would take three and Manx two, with Loganair taking a further two, but at a later date. In total, the order would amount to 13 aircraft, although many of them would be shuffled between the various operators over the coming five years as they were integrated into the fleet.

BM operated its final Viscount flight on 20th February 1988, 21 years after the airline had first acquired the type. We had time to fit out the first aircraft scheduled for delivery and paint it up in the new BM colour scheme in time to take it to Paris. This was an ideal time to present the aircraft to the aviation community and show that we were winning orders.

As a reward for our hard work, the management treated us to a night out in Paris at venues of our own choosing. My colleague and I chose Fouquet's restaurant, followed by the The Folies Bergère and a good time was had by all!

One of the important benefits of this deal was that the Isle of Man, courtesy of Manx Airlines, would now have aircraft based at the airport in Ronaldsway. This had not been the case previously and given that the island sits in the middle of the Irish Sea, it is subject to low visibility at certain times of the year, with low cloud in the winter and sea mist in the summer. Thus the first flights off the island were subject to the first flights onto the island being able to land.

With the introduction of the ATP, aircraft were now based on the island and given that the weather minima required for take-off is lower than that required for landing, the departing early flights were usually able to leave on time. This was particularly important to Manx Airlines, because the island's lower tax regime attracted many wealthy people who regularly used Concorde. In fact, I was told that after the south-east of England, the Isle of Man was, for a time, the biggest source of Concorde passengers, so it was always important that the Heathrow flight left on time.

Some final words about slots and their commercial importance. Following the sale of the ATPs, BM underwent further changes, buying and integrating other airlines which matched their route network and aspirations. In February 2007, BM bought British Mediterranean Airways (BMED), a British Airways franchise partner, and as a result gained access to new markets in Africa, the Middle East and Central Asia that were served by that carrier. As a condition of the sale, BM sold BMED's Heathrow slots to British Airways for £30 million.

In 2008 a decision by the EC (as it then was) to allow secondary slot trading by European airlines – basically buying and selling take-off and landing slots at congested airports –resulted in BM valuing its Heathrow slot holding at £770 million. Following this, BM was taken over by Lufthansa in October 2008. This was later agreed to by the European antitrust body in May 2009. However, in September 2011, Lufthansa announced that it intended to sell BM, following continued losses. Within three months, IAG (the parent company of BA) agreed to buy BM from Lufthansa for £172 million, thus increasing IAGs share of the slots at Heathrow from 45% to 53% and thereby ending BM's 74-year history.

The British Midland Viscounts stored at Tees-side, which we took in part-exchange for the ATPs. Note that the engines and propellers have already been removed. [Bob O'Brien]

Guidance in Guyana (1987)

In late October 1987 I had a trip planned to Brazil, but I was asked to call into Guyana on the way, principally because no-one had been to see Guyana Airways for a few years. They had bought two Series 2 748s in 1977, and apart from the initial product support, they had not had many visits from us during that time. The aircraft were mainly employed doing domestic flights and a 3x weekly service to Port-of-Spain in Trinidad. The airline was government-owned and domestic services were operated with a significant subsidy.

Guyana is very heavily forested; more than 80% of the country is covered in dense forest. Despite it being a former British Colony, it seems to be all but forgotten. It is the only English-speaking country in South America, though I suspect that few people could point to it accurately on a map. There were few decent roads and moving about was difficult, much of it being done on the many rivers I the country, hence the need for domestic flights to the more outlying areas.

I arrived in Georgetown and checked into the circular Pegasus Hotel on the outskirts of the city. The following day I was taken on a tour round the Guyana Airways facilities and had several meetings with the airline managers, all of whom were happy with the aircraft.

There was also a meeting with the Chief Pilot who, during the course of the conversation, asked me where my next destination was and what route I was taking. I was booked to go back to Miami and then take the overnight flight down to Rio. When I told him, he said, "Why don't you come with us to Lethem tomorrow and cross the border from there?"

My grasp of Guyana's geography was slight, to say the least, so we went over to the topographical maps on the operations room wall and he showed me where it was. It turned out that it is on the edge of the River Takutu, which forms the border between Guyana and Brazil. Knowing that it was unlikely that there would be any bridges, I asked, "How do you cross the river?"

He smiled, "There is a ferry service," he said, "but I'll check and make sure it's operating."

He then got on the HF (high-frequency) radio to Lethem. The telephone connections were unreliable and subject to damage from the occasional tropical storms, so they used the HF most of the time. They confirmed that it was working and he said, "I'll pick you up from your hotel at 10 tomorrow."

The airport is 25 miles out from the capital, which seems surprising, given that the capital is not big or densely populated, but apparently when the surveyors were looking for somewhere to build an airport, there was no suitable flat land in the immediate vicinity.

The following morning he collected me from the hotel. We drove to the airport, checked in and he went off to file the flight plan and check the Met conditions, while I had another wander around the hangar and chatted to some of the ground staff. The airline seemed very professional, despite operating in a remote area and under difficult conditions.

Once the formalities were completed we were soon airborne, heading for Lethem, along with about 25 passengers, six oil drums, and sundry amounts of plastic and steel construction materials and numerous other items – an average load, apparently! En route, it was just like flying over a huge green carpet, broken only as we passed over the Kaieteur Falls, a spectacular sight, and the world's largest single-drop waterfall. As a comparison, it is four times higher than Niagara Falls.

Unloading cargo, Guyana style. The 748 at Lethem. [Author]

Despite knowing Latin America quite well, it had not occurred to me that the airfield at Lethem would not have a paved runway and as I sat on the flight deck for final approach, I saw that in fact the runway was just a graded strip. A low pass ensured that it was free of grazing cattle, which was not always the case with such airfields, and we were cleared to land. As soon as the engines had stopped, the doors were opened and a swarm of people descended onto the airfield. It was at this point that I discovered that many of the passengers were Brazilians working in Guyana, some in the logging industry, and they were using the flight to return home.

Of course, it was a domestic flight, so no formalities and once having collected from the door of the aircraft, I said my 'thank yous' to the crew and joined several other people in a large American car which was the local communal taxi and took the short journey to the ferry, which turned out, not surprisingly perhaps, to be quite a rudimentary vessel. Basically, it was a timber-based pontoon with a large outboard motor at the stern. The crossing took just five minutes and we were soon on Brazilian territory in the small town of Bonfim, and then it was onto a large bus for the journey to the nearest large city of Boa Vista.

Brazil operates a huge bus network, similar in many ways to the Greyhound system in the US. The buses are comfortable, reliable, run on time and unusually in Latin America, are relatively accident-free.

The names of Brazilian towns and cities are certainly descriptive in their native language. Bonfim could be translated as 'wish' and Boa Vista means 'good view'. Other examples are Fortaleza (fort), Recife (reef) Salvador (saviour) and best of all perhaps, Rio de Janeiro (River of January). Rio does not stand on a river at all, rather on a huge bay, but the Portuguese explorers who discovered it in January 1502 were convinced that the bay was fed by a river.

So from the airport at Boa Vista it was the next flight to Brasilia, which would take about three hours and then a two-hour direct flight to Rio. If all this seems like a long journey, the alternative of going up to Miami – four hours flying – followed by the never-ending queues for immigration, only to leave the following day for the 9-hour flight to Rio wasn't a particularly attractive alternative. It also gave me the opportunity to see and understand more of both countries and saved the company some money on airfares!

Final approach to Lethem airfield Guyana, following a circuit to ensure that there were no cattle grazing in the area of the runway! [Author]

LAR & THE ATR (1988)

L inhas Aereas Regionais (LAR) was formed in 1988 as an independent airline with the intention of improving air services on the Iberian Peninsula. Following Portugal's accession to the EU in 1986, the TAP monopoly on routes out of Lisbon was at an end.

One of the more contentious pieces of TAP scheduling had been the Lisbon-Oporto route. The scheduling took no account of the needs of business traffic, with often the only flight of the day leaving and returning in the early afternoon. The train journey between the two cities, which are about 200 miles (320 km) apart took a minimum of five hours, so anyone doing business in either city was forced into a night-stop.

This was the era of the ATP (Advanced Turbo Prop), a 64-seat development of the 748. It was ideal for the shorter routes which LAR had planned to operate. On a sector length of one to one-and-a-half hours, there is actually no advantage in having a jet on the operation because it cannot complete the sector any more quickly than a turbo-prop. By the time the jet has climbed to its optimum cruising height and then descended at the other end, the amount of time spent in climbing and descending is greater than the turbo-prop, which will fly at a lower level. The difference in fuel burn is significant as well.

The management of LAR had connections with the management of SATA and felt that the ATP would be the right aircraft for their routes. This time there was none of the drama of bid and counter-bid, last-minute attempts by the competitor to upset the negotiations, or political interference. LAR was a private company and had raised money from its own resources.

Of course with the airline being completely new, the approach to providing spares and training is rather different, especially with completely new aircraft. The usual studies were made, but in this case, we were largely just confirming the careful route studies which LAR had already undertaken. We had a number of meetings with them and it was obvious that they had a clear vision of their strategy and how they would implement the introduction of the aircraft into service. They knew the aircraft anyway from their previous involvement with SATA, but they simply wanted to be sure that the ATP would be the most suitable aircraft for their network.

Having sought and obtained permission from the Portuguese Civil Aviation Authority, the first act by LAR was to introduce a thrice-daily service between Lisbon and Oporto at times which were built around business travel. The Faro route had also been poorly served, because like Oporto, TAP had treated it as an adjunct to their international services and LAR introduced daily sensibly-timed flights on this route as well.

Two aircraft were delivered in 1988 on a lease deal and immediately put into service on the two domestic routes. From the initial three flights a day, the frequency was increased to the point where there were a total of 22 flights a day between Lisbon and Oporto. Such was the popularity of the services that in 1990 a further ATP was ordered. Flights to other cities in Portugal followed, along with short-haul flights into Spanish and French cities which had not previously been served from Lisbon.

However, such was the success of the routes that another airline **Portugalia** appeared on the scene and the inevitable fare war began. As if this was bad enough, problems were beginning to appear with the ATP. There were numerous electrical problems and the undercarriage had to have various modifications in order to ensure that the propellers had sufficient ground clearance. As result of this, the aircraft became known within the aviation community as 'The Skoda' – after the Czech-built automobile notorious for its reliability problems at the time (which persisted until the company was bought by Volkswagen). This had a serious effect on LAR's reputation whilst Portugalia went from strength to strength. After five years, the aircraft were returned to BAe and LAR ceased operations.

The type was now into its fifth year of service and its reputation was going before it. Orders began to dry up and production was moved to BAe's factory at Prestwick in Scotland in an attempt to reduce production costs. Various attempts were made to improve the aircraft, together with a PR tactic of changing the name to Jetstream 61 for aircraft produced at Prestwick, but to no avail, because by now, its main competitors, the ATR 72 and the De Havilland Canada Dash 8 had become well established with short-haul airline operators and were winning almost all the contracts.

An attempt by BAe to integrate with ATR in Toulouse, was attempted, but ATR, realising they had the lion's share of the market by now, did not show much interest in the idea. Only 64 ATP aircraft were completed. When their production stopped it effectively marked the end of large-scale airliner production in the UK.

The Turkmenistan government 125 on arrival at Ashkhabad from its delivery flight. [Author]

The BAe 125 arriving for a demo at Elista in southern Russia [author]

Turkmenistan Tales (1991-92)

The year was 1991 and I was working in the sales department of the Corporate Jets Division of BAe. My boss called me into his office one Monday morning and said, "Sit down... would you like some coffee?" so I knew I wasn't in trouble at least. After the coffee had been poured he said, "You know Russia, don't you? I've got a job for you; we've got a new agent I'd like you to look at. How soon can you go to Moscow?" It was like a scene from a James Bond movie. The Berlin wall had come down, Russia was suddenly the centre of attention and I didn't need to visit Gypsy Rose Lee to foresee travel to foreign parts! And so it was to Russia I flew – with brochures and, of course, a visa.

With the help of the Russian and British embassies we had identified a newly-formed company at Moscow's main international airport at Sheremetyevo, north of Moscow, who were willing, and it seemed, able, to help us. They were about to launch an air taxi service using one of our leased-in BAe 125 executive jets, for which we first had to get certification. Eventually, after much to-ing and fro-ing this was done and in the meantime a lot of interest had evolved, so it was all systems go.

We had initially looked only at Russia as a future market, but it soon became apparent that there were other interested former Soviet Union countries, too. Just as I was leaving from one visit, the agent asked me to prepare for a visit to Turkmenistan next time we were there, because they were interested in one of our new 1000 Series business jets, which was larger and had a longer range than previous models.

The first thing I did when I was back at Hatfield was to get the atlas out to see where Turkmenistan was! After many faxes and phone calls, the visit was finally set up. We were to fly to Moscow, meet up with the agent and then fly on to Ashkabad (as it was then known). We arrived in Moscow early one evening, joined the inevitable one-hour queue for immigration and KGB check and then walked just round the corner to the Novotel, and a room with an excellent view of the airport.

The following morning we were collected from the hotel and taken to the agent's office, which was in a hangar on the other side of the airfield. Initially, I had assumed we were there for a briefing and then to catch the Aeroflot flight from Terminal 1 (the domestic terminal) but it transpired that we were flying direct from the office – in a big Russian-built IL-18 four-engined turboprop! But this was no ordinary IL-18 – it was an IL-18D to be precise and belonged to a company called GosNiiGa which, until a few months previously, had been the state research organisation and the aircraft had regularly flown to the Arctic, so we made a mental note to keep an eye on the landscape on the way there!

The aircraft was full of monitoring equipment but there was a sort of 'lounge' area towards the rear of the fuselage and this was to be our home for the next four and a half hours as we droned down to Ashkabad. The fact that it had a magnetometer unit underneath made it look like a bomber, which amused all concerned, but this also meant that its cruising speed was a bit slower.

On reaching Ashkabad, we were collected from the airport in a Soviet-era minibus and it soon became clear that life in Turkmenistan had changed very little from the old Soviet way. The hotel, too, was pure Soviet-era, and their system was still in place at reception, too. Hand in your passport and you're given a release note to go to a particular floor. On each floor is a large table, behind which is a woman with a face like a bulldog chewing a wasp. I was not to be intimidated by this however, because previous experience of Soviet hotels had taught me that these were possibly the most important people in the hotel. A few small gifts, bars of western chocolate for example, and the world was at your feet. I will explain more later. In the meantime small rooms, small single beds, a TV that looked as if it had been made by John Logie Baird and a shower that produced water which looked like Brown Windsor soup.

Thankfully, the only time we ate in the hotel was at breakfast; it was continental style, with bread and assorted meats and cheeses on trays. However, the local flies were well aware of this and had easy access via the open windows. We were convinced that they actually went into a holding pattern once the food had appeared. Only tea without milk was available in those strange cups without handles – at least we assumed they had never had handles – perhaps they'd just broken off! We never did find one which didn't have a crack in it.

The following day, we had a meeting with the Oil and Gas Ministry, who were the nominal purchasers of the aircraft, though it would normally be used by the President's Office. The Oil and Gas Ministry was the most powerful organisation in the country, simply because it made so much money. Turkmenistan is the fourth-largest supplier of natural gas in the world. The oil and gas ministry was run by the vice-president of the country and it was into his office we were shown. The usual pleasantries took place and we began the discussion.

The VP was actually Russian and didn't speak any English but the agent had brought two excellent interpreters with us from Moscow. After the general discussions, we got down to the question of price. A guy who was clearly the CFO, since he had the largest calculator I've ever seen, pumped the numbers into it and said to the VP, "*That's about 7 days' gas supply.*" I don't speak fluent Russian but I knew enough to understand what had been said. It became apparent that this was the way they calculated everything, since they'd been tied to an unconvertible rouble for so long and at that point still did not have a currency of their own. However, their calculations assumed greater significance when it became apparent that what they wanted to do was sell us a quantity of gas equivalent to the deal. This is not unusual, and is known as counter-trade, but often it becomes enormously complicated. We finished the meeting and went back to the hotel to consider our options. We tried to send a telex back to the UK to alert them, but it wasn't possible, because the hotel was not able to use it for international traffic. There was only one phone in the whole hotel; international calls were limited and had to be booked six hours in advance. This was to prove very frustrating, as I shall describe later.

So it was back on the 'bomber' to Moscow, and overnight at the airport hotel and back to the UK. The next day we had a meeting with the contracts guys, in order to explain what had taken place. They winced but said it was do-able. We also had to arrange a demo flight. At the time, we had two of the -1000 series aircraft available as demonstrators:

Aircraft registration G-ELRA (extra long range aircraft) was in the US and G-LRBJ (long-range business jet) was in South Africa, so we had to 'borrow' one that was coming off the production line and hastily register it. As with cars, the Civil Aviation Authority in the UK will allow you to have any registration you want, provided you are willing to pay the administration charge, it has not been used before, or is offensive. So we took G-BUIX (nothing clever about that, it was just the next on the register!) and set off back to Ashkabad, with a stop in Moscow as protocol demanded and to pick up the interpreters.

At that time, Ashkabad was not an international airport. Under the Soviet system customs and immigration could only be performed at major Russian airports, so a flight from Moscow to one of the 'stans' for example was actually a domestic flight. Bizarrely, you could fly out internationally, but inbound you had to come in via an entry point, and all the former Soviet airspace was still covered by the Russian military, so in order to keep things nice and tidy with diplomatic clearances, we flew in via Moscow.

On the way back from Ashkabad we were asked to do a demonstration, which turned out to be to the breakaway Chechen government, so we stopped at Elista in southern Russia on the way, to do a demonstration. Grozny was just a few hundred kilometres away. They were apparently interested in a reliable aircraft that could get them as far away from Chechnya as quickly as possible. Hardly surprising, given the circumstances at the time.

The Turkmenistan demo went well and discussions advanced rapidly. The aircraft returned to Ashkabad to drop us off and continue negotiations. After one particular meeting we returned to the hotel in order to make a phone call back to Hatfield. We booked the call and were told to go to our room and wait. I had previously called on my Russian negotiating skills with the *babushka* (old lady) on our floor desk. She had let us use a larger room at the end of the floor as a working and chill-out room free of charge. She also produced some very decent sandwiches and a samovar and we settled back for the wait.

Eventually the knock came to the door with a shout of *"Telefon, telefon"*. My colleague leapt up and set off down the stairs – there were no lifts in the hotel – as fast as he could. A few minutes later he was back – with a very long face. They had only allowed five minutes for the call and it had taken him almost that long to get to reception and by the time he'd been put through to the office, the operators in Moscow, through which all calls were routed in those days, had pulled the plug on our five-minute allocated call. The interpreters learned some new English swear-words that afternoon! Fortunately, we were leaving for Moscow later that day and with a three-hour time difference, we were able to put a call back to the office in from the hotel there without any problem.

Back in the UK, negotiations on the gas sale had moved ahead and a draft contract had been prepared. Time to get on a plane to Moscow again, which we did – in the company of the BBC's chief news correspondent Kate Adie and a film crew. I've always found it rather disconcerting to be on the same plane as a war correspondent; I once found myself on the same flight as ITV's Julian Manyon heading for some trouble spot in the Middle East, but this time Kate Adie and her crew were heading for Chechnya and we weren't.

The next day we were off to Ashkabad again and back to the hotel from hell; this time it was a GosNiiGa Russian jet TU-134 so our flight time was significantly quicker than last time! Good progress with the deal, and then suddenly, to our surprise, they said "Look, let's forget all this counter-trade stuff, we'll pay in cash. Will you accept deutschmarks?"

The Turkmenis had been supplying gas directly to East Germany for years through a huge pipeline but, instead of the roubles they had previously received, they were now being paid in West German marks, which at the time was a very strong and convertible currency. Our response caused us to have to explain later to the interpreters the meaning of the expression, "Is the Pope Catholic?"

A draft contract was signed and a 33% deposit arrived in the Corporate Jets bank about a week later.

We repeated the same trip a few weeks later, signed the contract and headed home, via a Moscow which by now had now become party-town central, with no less than three Irish pubs and any number of interesting night spots in the process. It was helpful that the flight back to London the following day was an early evening one! Off up to the factory in Chester a few days later for a discussion with them about build programmes, delivery dates and interiors. At this point the Turkmenis had plans and suggestions about interior fittings and colour schemes, but had not finalised their ideas and were planning to visit the factory within a month for final discussions. We allocated an aircraft for delivery in November 1992. The visit took place by the officials from Turkmenistan and the interior and exterior details were finalised. If you're buying your own executive jet, there is no standard fit as such and thus no limit, other than weight and space, as to how you configure the interior. You can have any colour, size or shape of seat, whatever colours for the walls and carpets and if you would prefer a bar to a galley, that's just fine.

Actually, the interior the Turkmenis chose was very functional, but about right for the job it was supposed to do, in contrast to some of those we'd supplied to other heads of government. We received the second stage payment on time, and the final payment was made a month early – the first time that had ever happened, apparently.

Only one problem remained – every country in the world has a unique registration identifier. At this time, Turkmenistan didn't have its own allocated registration. All their current aircraft had Soviet markings. They had applied to the International Civil Air Organisation (ICAO) for their own unique registration prefix to be issued, but had not had a reply. By now, they had set up their own aviation authority and made it clear to ICAO that as a newly-independent nation they did not want the 125 or the Boeing 757 they had on order for their new airline to be placed on the Russian register under any circumstances, even temporarily.

Normally, a new aircraft is collected by the customer, not least because the delivery flight gives all concerned the opportunity to familiarise themselves with the aircraft. However, given the circumstances, it was agreed that we would register the aircraft in the UK and deliver it with a UK registration. The aircraft would be de-registered on arrival in Turkmenistan though, and they would not be allowed to use it until the new prefix had been allocated. ICAO issued the new prefix just a couple of weeks later, but apparently, there was some sort of mix-up over the initial registration. The final registration was EZ-B021, but initially it was applied as EK-B021. The EK- prefix had been allocated to Armenia, although no-one seemed to have noticed. The fact that there is a 'K' but no 'Z' in the Russian alphabet may have been a contributory factor!

In summing up the whole experience, it was a very unusual deal. Every aspect of the negotiations was different from those we had done before and the circumstances under which we working were quite trying. Even in the old days, you could walk freely around any of the big cities in the Soviet Union if you had some free time, but we weren't allowed outside the hotel without a minder and any 'excursions' had to be arranged in advance and usually consisted of being driven around town in a creaking Gaz minibus with curtains on the windows. We taken to visit a carpet factory one day, where teenage girls were weaving rugs, but that was about it. We were taken out to dinner in the evenings and the food was quite good. There were no cinemas though and only two TV stations, both transmitting in Russian. We usually managed about a week before 'cabin fever' set in.

Despite it being a nominally Muslim country, there was no problem with alcohol; that is until the night we celebrated the signing of the deal and one of the colleagues had a little more vodka than was good for him. Each one of us had to make a short speech and propose a toast. He was one of the last to perform and his speech was slurred to the point where he was becoming very difficult to understand. Fortunately for her, one of the interpreters was sitting next to me. She nudged me in the ribs and asked me to translate into intelligible English, so that she in turn, could translate into Russian.

The following morning, a little the worse for wear, we fought the flies at breakfast time and headed for the airport to our 'private' Tupolev to take us back to Moscow. It was a quiet flight back, but by the time we reached Moscow, we had largely recovered and were able to make a passable attempt at a celebration party that evening.

Back in the office, we used to have a scoreboard which had a bell over the top. Every time a contract was signed, the bell would be rung and the numbers changed rather like a cricket scoreboard. It was a very satisfying feeling.

We took a smaller version of the 125 to the Moscow Air Show in 1992. The show was held at Zhukovsky airfield, the former Soviet flight test centre hidden in a large forest, one and a half hours' drive south of Moscow. This was the first time there had ever been a show of this type and given the interest in business jets in Russia it seemed appropriate to take an aircraft for everyone to see.

The airfield itself is huge and has one of the world's longest runways at 17,000 feet (5,400m). The airfield was also used as a test site for the Soviet *Buran* Spacecraft, which bore a more than passing resemblance to the US Space Shuttle. The secondary runway had been set aside for the static park and parked there was possibly the strangest collection of aircraft I have ever seen, including one with an enormous hydrogen tank on top of the fuselage.

We had long ago learned that aircraft are never sold at air shows, however the publicity which both the air show and the aircraft attract is worth the cost and effort. This being the first such air show, it was extremely well attended by business, the military and the general public, no doubt helped by some very fine weather.

The 125 was the only western aircraft at the show and naturally attracted a lot of attention. In fact, within an hour of the show opening we were approached by Channel 1, the biggest TV channel in Russia, to do a feature on the aircraft. We had just finished that when Rossiya 1 arrived to do a similar feature. Amusingly, their first question was, "What sort of feature did Channel 1 do?" so that they could do something different. They wanted to concentrate on the flight deck and a power unit was quickly found, and hooked up to the aircraft in order to show the instruments operating. The aircraft had an 'electronic' flight deck and they seemed fascinated by the colours on the display screens. Apparently both channels ran the features on TV that night, although we didn't see them.

'62 Black' or Russian Roulette (1992)

In May 1992 we had a sales trip planned to Moscow. A week before, I got a phone call from our agent there, asking me if we could arrive a couple of days earlier. It seemed that he had identified a potential customer – Ноябрьск нефтегазовая (or **Noyabrsk Oil & Gas Company** to you and me), in Siberia who wanted to buy a couple of 125s. That was fine in principle, but as ever, there was a snag. The company concerned had bought two used Gulfstream II 12-seater business jets, built by Grumman Aircraft in the US, and fitted with Rolls-Royce engines. The aircraft had a good reputation but the operator had discovered that operating them from the middle of Siberia was not as easy as they had first thought.

So off we went, myself and our man who was a particular expert on used business jets, courtesy of British Airways, to Sheremetyevo airport for an overnight at the nearby Novotel, with its complementary views of the airport apron and Ruddle's beer on draught – and no, I have no idea why either, but it was excellent!

The next morning, booted and suited, we were waiting outside the hotel, enjoying the warm spring weather, when the agent's driver turned up with a minibus. Seeing us in our suits, he said,

"You have coats with you?"

"No," we answered. "Lovely weather isn't it?"

"Here, it is – in Noyabrsk it's minus 15."

Noyabrsk, for those of you have never heard of it – and we hadn't– is a Siberian town on the Arctic Circle. It's a major oil extraction and pumping station on the trans-Siberian oil pipeline, but it's not the easiest place to get to – about three days by train, so we 'borrowed' the agent's 125 and flew there in three hours. We had realised that none of the interpreters were coming with us on this trip, and we were about to discover why.

We arrived to piles of snow everywhere, 2 metres high in places, and the forecast -15C was correct, so it was quickly out of the aircraft and into the accommodation.

Ah yes, the accommodation... It can best be described as 'rustic', with no curtains on the windows, completely overheated and being so far north, it did not go dark at night in May. Those eyeshades the airlines give you come in really useful at times...

The people we wanted to see were out of town and not expected back until the following day, so we sat down and went through the log books. It was clear the aircraft had done very little flying in recent months and there had been little maintenance. Both were on the US register, being N7PQ and N8PQ respectively, (about which more later), the Gulfstream II not having been airworthiness-approved at that time for operations in Russia. However, the Russian Civil Aviation Authority were pushing for them to be certificated, which would be a long and expensive process and Gulfstream were not prepared to support it. In addition, the air-worthiness certificates were rapidly running out anyway. Democracy had dawned in Russia by then and the local media were asking what these aircraft were doing hanging around the airport all this time, hence the reason for them being up for sale.

On the following day, the directors arrived and we were finally able to inspect the aircraft. Large fur-lined and hooded jackets and gloves had been found for us, but it was impossible to get any normal steps near the aircraft because they were parked on a tax-iway from which the snow had not been removed, so a bit of lateral thinking was required. We borrowed a ladder from the fire service and with two sturdy fireman holding the bottom, we were able to enter the aircraft. The interiors seemed fine, as did the flight deck, but the lack of maintenance and the fact that they had been left outside during a Siberian winter were a worry. During the whole time we were there, we never saw or heard a movement on the airfield. Apart from the two GIIs and our 125, the only other aircraft on the airfield were two utility aircraft, well wrapped up against the Siberian weather.

We left later that day for Moscow and with the time difference, arrived in time to make a phone call to the UK to discuss the trade-in value of the GIIs. Later the following day we received a fax from Hatfield which contained an offer for the GIIs against a couple of used 125-800s. The fax was transmitted on to Noyabrsk via the agent, but we never heard from them again. Later enquiries revealed that they were not impressed with the trade-in value we had offered for their aircraft. Anyone who has ever traded-in their old car will be all too familiar with that scenario!

We heard some time later that both the aircraft had been moved from Noyabrsk, and here comes the mysterious bit. I had a meeting with the head of the Russian CAA a few months later about a totally unrelated matter and asked him what had happened to them. Apparently N8PQ had been ferried back to the US, but he said that N7PQ, constructor's number 62, had acquired the radio call-sign '62 BLACK'.

"What does that mean?" I asked.

We were speaking in English, but I thought I had misunderstood him, so we switched to Russian.

"шестьдесят два черный" (sixty-two black), he repeated. "It's been adopted by the Russian Air Force."

By now I was really intrigued. He couldn't add very much, so I asked another contact, who worked at Zhukovsky, the Russian aviation test site near Moscow, and the home of the TU-144 'Konkordski', about the story. He made some enquiries and discovered that it had been flown to the huge Air Force base at Chkalovsky outside Moscow.

Apparently it was being used as a VIP transport for the military and the call-sign reflected the fact that it was not actually integrated into the air force and was probably still carrying the US registration.

The blackened Russian White House following the events of September 1993. [Author]

I did visit Chkalovsky twice during this time, but I never saw the GII.

"Black" in government parlance invariably means deniable (e.g. 'black ops') so I suppose the call-sign was entirely appropriate. As in English, the Russian word for black has strong connotations and can be used to mean anything unpleasant; black mood, black day, etc. Neither aircraft was painted black when we saw them at Noyabrsk.

Subsequently I was able to contact a senior member of the Russian Civil Aviation Authority who told me that he had issued a directive and banned commercial flights of the GII in Russia. This caused a lot of problems and he was invited to talk to the government and asked to cancel the directive. These were people who were apparently connected with the owners but their requests had been ignored.

At Chkalovsky airfield, an official company began to operate, performing transportation services for the Ministry of Defence. Everything seemed to be legitimate until the unit suddenly started commercial operations. After some time, the issue was settled and there was no further action. However, when they flew abroad they occasionally had problems, since the aircraft was still carrying its US registration. Because of this, the oil company then officially transferred the GII to the Unit; however no transfer title or lease documents were ever seen. But when the oil company learned of the original directive, the aircraft was grounded.

Some time after this, a very famous test pilot, who had been awarded many medals apparently came to the Civil Aviation Authority to ask to allow them to allow commercial flights with the aircraft. Despite being a senior test pilot, all explanations of certification standards and the need for international cooperation did not impress him. He said that he knew and understood what was necessary, but when people do not get salaries, and they have nothing to eat, the standards are not that important.

A way out was suggested to them by declaring the GII as a State aircraft. It would not allow them to sell tickets, but they would be able to fly specialists to major cities, factories, and government meetings, and to receive money from the companies into their own bank account.

For a while, apparently, they followed the advice and nothing more was heard from them. Then suddenly there was a cable from the airport in Ekaterinburg saying that a GII had landed there and they were trying to sell tickets for flights on the aircraft, completely against the authority they had been given. Following this a ban was placed on commercial flights for all GIIs. The aircraft was taken out of service and stored.

Sometime after this, the aircraft was flown from Russia. It is not known where it went or how long it was kept for. Apparently it reappeared on the books of a US broker almost six years later, but there appears to have been no other owner during that time.

Was it in storage somewhere, or was it being used? Perhaps we shall never know.

A Tale of Two Stans (1993-94)

Following on from the success of the sale to Turkmenistan, we decided to venture further east, and explore the sales possibilities in two of Central Asia's largest countries, Uzbekistan and Kazakhstan. Contacts were made and demonstrations were set up.

It was now 1993 and the large cities in Russia were rapidly embracing capitalism. New buildings were being constructed, old ones were being refurbished. Suddenly there were private cars on the roads; kiosks selling everything from paperbacks to beer appeared on the pavements. However, the further east you went, as we had discovered in Turkmenistan, the slower the pace of change.

Our first trip was to Tashkent, Uzbekistan's capital. We were only there for a few days – it was actually an extension of a larger demo we were doing in Turkey, but we travelled by scheduled flight from London and arrived via Moscow, as protocol demanded, since there was no formal immigration or customs system in either country at the time. We also needed to pick up the support staff. No problems there, through security and into a Vaz minibus for the journey to the hotel. I asked where we were staying and I was told it would be the Intourist. This filled me with foreboding, because I knew the one in Moscow only too well, and it was one of the grubbiest, least appealing hotels I had ever stayed in, not exactly enhanced by the prostitutes and their leather-jacketed pimps who used to hang around the lobby. Only a few years earlier, a night watchman at the hotel had hacked two Swedish visitors to death on the steps of the hotel in broad daylight and in April 1999, a few years after our visit, a bomb exploded in a lift in the hotel and a number of people were injured. No explanation was ever given for this.

The one in Tashkent was built in a similar style (Intourist was the Soviet travel organisation) and we went through the usual formalities of dealing with reception and then the floor dragon on our allocated floor.

My worst thoughts were confirmed. The public areas were poorly-lit, as were the rooms. The carpets were stained and sticky and there were broken and missing tiles in the bathroom and shower areas. The bed was a small single with a rudimentary cover. Clearly some inducement to sleep was going to be necessary during this visit. I went down the corridor to my colleague, who after our last experience in Turkmenistan, had brought a Sat Phone, so that we could maintain regular contact with the UK. It was a cumbersome object, about the size of a record player, but worth its weight in gold. He fired it up and within a minute was telling Hatfield that we'd arrived safely, when I spotted a movement on the floor. 'Here we go', I thought. Dirty carpets, broken tiles, poorly lit and cleaned rooms and despite us being on one of the upper floors, it was cockroach heaven.

Several appeared at once and I began to kill them with my shoe, making a loud banging noise on the flimsy carpet each time, but more followed. My colleague was asked by the guy on the other end of the phone if there was building work going on in the hotel, but he said, "No – it's just Barry killing cockroaches."

Cockroaches had long been in a problem in Soviet hotels, brought about by a poor cleaning regime (they rarely used vacuum cleaners, just a sweeping brush for the carpets and a dirty mop in the bathroom), and it was the habit of people staying in hotels during that era to bring their own food. Restaurants were expensive by their standards and only used for special occasions, which meant they were frequented by large groups and thus tended to fill up very quickly. There were relatively few, even in major cities, so the whole problem of eating when away from home was compounded several times over. The result was that people often brought their own food and the crumbs which accumulated from the guests, coupled with the poor lighting, made them a des-res for members of the *Blattodea* family, who took full advantage of the conditions.

I returned to my room and switched on the light as I entered, and sure enough several of them scuttled away into the dark corners. It wasn't long before they re-appeared though and my shoe was put to good use again. We had a word with the interpreter, who of course had the same problem, but was more used to these unwelcome visitors. She went to reception and complained, saying that we were foreign guests, which would normally mean special treatment, but they simply said that the hotel was full. She also tried several shops looking for insect repellent, but there was none to be found. Clearly the hotel hadn't bought it all, because by the following morning I had killed 25 and laid them out neatly on some toilet paper on the desk, in the hope that the maid might put down some powder or other treatment. However, when I returned later in the day, they were still there; actually, it was difficult to tell whether the room had been cleaned or not. We did speak to the agent about another hotel, but his prognosis was that there wasn't a better – or cleaner – hotel in town, and sadly I think he was right.

Having set up the demo to the transport department of the Uzbek government, we performed it the following day, to everyone's apparent satisfaction, and returned to cockroach castle. The following morning we had another meeting with the Ministry of Transport, following which I decided to go for a ride on the excellent metro system in the city. There is one particular station, *Kosmonavtov* – a specially decorated metro station to celebrate an Uzbek astronaut. I had my camera with me and was about to take a photo when, from out of nowhere, an armed security guard appeared and asked me to put the camera away. I was told later that apparently the Uzbek government regard their metro as a military installation and photography is forbidden.

When it came time to leave, we paid the bills, and asked for the bills for the interpreter.

"They must pay their own bills," we were told. She was still in her room, so I went up and gave her some dollars and while we were loading the bags, she went to the check-out desk. A few minutes later, she came out to where we were loading the minibus.

"Because I'm Russian, they won't let me pay in dollars – it has to be in som," she told us.

Som was the local currency.

"Well, there's a bank in the lobby isn't there?"

"Yes, but they haven't got any money."

Now this particular lady was a bit of a joker and I thought this was a typical example of her humour, but she insisted it wasn't. I went to the bank and asked if I could change money and the sour-faced teller, doubtless sick of answering the same old question said, "No money until evening."

A bank with no money – well that was a first! We had neither the time nor the inclination to hang around any longer and I didn't fancy the idea of an attractive young woman wandering around the streets of Tashkent with several hundred dollars in her handbag, so I went off to find the nearest foreign currency kiosk. I returned to the hotel, som in hand, and was about to give the cash to her, when she shied away from me.

"What's wrong?" I asked.

"You can't just give me the money in the lobby like that," she said, "people will think I'm a prostitute."

"OK, so what do we do, go outside?"

"NO! That's even worse! But I have an idea. I'll buy a magazine, give it to you and you can put the money inside."

She had some small change, so I went off to buy some coffees while she bought a magazine and came to the café table. During the conversation and in the hope that none of the men in ill-fitting suits who were inhabiting the café were paying attention, I feigned a brief glimpse through its pages, inserted the money into the magazine and passed it back to her. After a suitable interval she went to the loo, removed the money from the magazine, then reappeared at the reception desk and paid the bill in the requisite som. Finally, we were ready to leave!

We didn't sell the 125 executive jet to the Uzbeks. However, they did show interest in having a larger aircraft in full VIP configuration, plus another two standard aircraft to perform the popular internal tourist routes in the 'Golden Triangle – Tashkent, Bukhara & Samarkand – and closer destinations such as Almaty. It occurred to me that there was a possibility for sales so I passed all the details on to my colleagues in the Commercial Aircraft division. I am pleased to say that three of these aircraft were later sold to **Uzbekistan Airways** and have been in service since they were delivered in 1997 re-branded as RJ85s, so some good came from our original visit – eventually!

This was October 1993 and there was increasing tension in Moscow. On the way down, the interpreter had been explaining that there had been increasing amounts of unrest on the streets, brought about by a constitutional crisis within the government. Boris Yeltsin had dissolved Parliament by force, but the parliamentarians were having none of it. The agent was with us in Tashkent and he too had been monitoring the situation, not least because a few days later we were due to sign a contract for the sale of a used 125 in Moscow. The interpreter had called friends back in Moscow and they had confirmed that moving about was difficult and road blocks had been set up.

Earlier in the day and unknown to us because a news blackout had been imposed, the main TV station at Ostankino on the northern outskirts of Moscow had been attacked by the rebels and more than 180 people had been killed and injured. Fighting had broken out on the streets of Moscow, which had brought about a curfew that, by all accounts, was being strictly enforced.

The demonstrator aircraft was due to go back to the UK later that day, but when we tried to file a flight plan for our return to Moscow, we were told that, because of the crisis, no private aircraft were being allowed in or out and there was no indication of when this might change. The demo crew elected to return via Istanbul. Subsequently we learned that a curfew would be imposed in Moscow that evening at 2300. This applied even to the Metro, though in those days it was not easy even to reach central Moscow by train from Domodedovo Airport, where our flight would arrive and which was a long way south of Moscow. There were no hotels at all in the vicinity of the airport.

Only one commercial flight was scheduled to return to Moscow that night, but it would arrive just as the curfew came into operation. The agent had arranged for a car to collect us and take us into the centre. However, the driver, having negotiated a number of roadblocks on the way out to the airport, was less than enthusiastic about returning to the centre and suggested that we sleep in the car until the curfew was lifted at 6am. However, the interpreter, knowing that we were due to sign an important deal the following day, was having none of it. She eventually persuaded the driver that even with roadblocks, the drive back to Moscow was preferable to four of us spending the night sleeping in a Volga saloon, so we set off.

Between leaving the airport and arriving in the centre at our hotel, our interpreter negotiated no less than 12 roadblocks, getting out of the car each time to explain to the OMON personnel manning the checkpoints that we were foreign guests and needed to reach the hotel. OMON translates roughly as special purpose mobility unit and they wear different uniforms from both the police and the military, but are ranked somewhere in between the two. They are not to be messed with and we admired the tact and diplomacy with which she managed our transit through the newly-erected barriers. Our reception at each one varied greatly, from a casual wave through once the passports had been shown, to a full-blown examination of the car, us and the baggage we were carrying, all of which, it is fair to say, were carried out politely and efficiently.

Finally we made it to the hotel, where, after a short discussion, we booked the interpreter a room. We felt that to leave her and the driver to negotiate their way to their homes was simply asking for trouble, given the palpable tension on the streets, particularly in central Moscow. The driver was still sulking from having to drive through the checkpoints and decided nevertheless to return home. By now it was 2am, and the hotel bar was closed, so we went straight to my room for a couple of celebratory beers from the mini bar.

The following day we signed the contract in Moscow, followed by a vodka-fuelled lunch punctuated with much toasting, and headed to the airport for the British Airways flight back to London. On the way, we passed the Russian White House, its interior completely destroyed and the upper floors covered in smoke from the fires which had raged within, brought about by the tank-shelling. It was clearly a good time to be leaving.

A few months later, we headed in a similar direction, this time a little further east, to Alma Ata in Kazakhstan. Again, the obligatory stop in Moscow for interpreters and supplies and to file a flight plan. This one was slightly more complicated than previously, because we would be flying near – but definitely not over – the Baikonour Cosmodrome. We had applied to fly at 40,000 feet (for better fuel economy) but were told that we would not be allowed to fly above 32,000 feet because, they said, their radar would not be able to see us. We tried to negotiate, but to no avail. Air Traffic Control was provided by the military and rules were rules. Our flight plan was finally agreed and the next morning we set off for the four-and-a-half hour flight to Alma Ata.

All flights normally follow a set of way-points or beacons. The beacons are read by the aircraft's on-board navigation systems and the aircraft under normal circumstances will fly from one beacon to another. Some are imaginary, but in the days of the post-Soviet

Union, the beacons were fixed points on the ground – or so we thought. As we tracked eastwards, we followed the allocated track until at one point, not too far from Baikonour, the aircraft veered slightly to the right and began to head towards the next beacon. At this point, air traffic control called us and said, "India X-ray, you are 10 degrees right of track – resume normal navigation." I volunteered to go back and check the wing tips, to ensure that we weren't being shadowed by a couple of MiGs! We thought that somehow the navigation system had missed the beacon, but later discussions revealed that in fact the beacon was a radio transmitter on the back of a military truck. Apparently, for reasons best known to themselves, it was not uncommon for the trucks to be moved around and we were told that the truck had probably been moved from its original position.

Although Kazakhstan is the world's seventh largest country, much of it is desert. What lies below it are some very rare minerals. Aside from oil and gas, this country probably contains more members of the periodic table ending in -ium than any other country on earth. Kazakhstan is the size of Western Europe. However, it's remoteness and it's very low population density – only 17 million people live in the country – mean that transport and communications are very basic.

We landed in Alma Ata, which at the time was still the capital, and headed for the hotel. Plans were under way to build an entirely new city, to be called Astana, to the north of Alma Ata, which sits directly above a set of tectonic plates and is thus prone to earthquakes. Astana would then then replace Alma Ata as the capital and Alma Ata would revert to its original name of Almaty.

The hotel was very different from the one in Tashkent. I suspect it had been a large guest-house for Communist party members previously, because it looked smart and well-organised. No floor dragons here – just a reception desk and directions to the rooms, which were clean and airy. It was being used mainly by foreign oil workers, who had been brought in to advise on Kazakhstan's oil extraction and refining systems. The food was good too.

The demonstrations took place as arranged and everyone seemed satisfied with what we were able to offer. However, given the sheer size of Kazakhstan, the government felt that it would be more appropriate to have a bigger aircraft, which not only would have more seats, but also a longer range. However, their minds were by no means made up, and we agreed to return again in a couple of months' time.

Then, it was back to Moscow. None of the check-out dramas we had experienced in Tashkent and four-and-half hours later we touched down at Sheremetyevo Airport. This time Moscow was back to its peaceful self and business people from all over the world were descending on Moscow to take advantage of the *perestroika* (restructuring) which had made doing business with Russia so much easier. This was all very well, but the limited hotel accommodation in Moscow at that time meant that rooms were hard to find and we found ourselves overnighting in the dreaded Intourist hotel in the centre of the city. The floor dragons had been replaced by prostitutes, who seemed to be everywhere – even in the lifts, and we hastily headed to our rooms to compare cockroach counts. I was tasked with finding a decent restaurant for us to have dinner. By this time many new ones had sprung up. So, after some decent Italian food and a few beers, we headed back to our rooms. If there was any chocolate on the pillow, it would have probably have been leftovers from the previous guest.

The Intourist hotel, having been built in the Brezhnev era of the 1970s, was eventually demolished in 2002 and replaced by the 5-star Ritz-Carlton, which is perhaps an example of the pace at which change was taking place in Russia at the time.

Sochi Sojourn (1994)

By 1994 Corporate Jets had been taken over by the Cruise Missile manufacturer Raytheon, 125 production had been moved to the US and most of the UK-based staff had been made redundant. Fortunately, I was able to move back to the airliner side of the business, where the 146 was still selling well. Again, I found myself looking at new markets in the former Soviet Union. In Russia, we had put forward a plan to the Aviation Ministry to operate a shuttle service between Moscow and the newly re-named St Petersburg (formerly Leningrad). Transaero, the first private airline of any size to begin operations in Russia after *glasnost* (openness) had set up a subsidiary called Transaero Express who were very interested in opening such a route and Moscow had a little-used down-town airport known as *Centralni,* which although it had a short runway, was certainly long enough for a 146 operation. All the airports in Moscow are a long way from the city centre, and with a booming economy and many foreign business visitors, there was a lot of potential traffic between the two cities. Coincidentally, four of the largest Russian aviation companies were located close to this airfield. Aeroflot did operate flights to St Petersburg, but they were not timed for business traffic and the alternative was a 6-hour overnight train journey on which, at the time, robberies were common. Pulkovo Airport in St Petersburg is close to the centre of town, so with a flying time between the two of just over an hour, day return trips for business would entirely feasible.

Together with Transaero Express, we had a series of meetings with the Aviation Ministry and the idea was generally well received. We did the usual route studies with Transaero Express and after a number of meetings, they agreed that all the numbers made sense. Transaero then asked if we would do several demonstration flights, to prove the validity of their case. We agreed to this and they set about getting permissions. A couple of weeks later, I returned to Moscow, but the news was not good. The Aviation Ministry had refused permission for us to use *Centralni* on the basis that it was 'unsafe' and that flying was not allowed near city centres. The second part was certainly true. Apparently, the thing which most appalled the top brass when Mathias Rust landed his light aircraft in Red Square in 1987 was the fact that he'd flown over the city in order to land there. We went back and argued the case, but they were having none of it.

It so happened that one of the interpreters we had used in the past lived in a block of flats which overlooked the airfield. I called her for a chat and she told me that there were rumours the airfield was to be closed and sold off for private development. This made a lot of sense, as it was very conveniently located, with a Metro station just across the road, bizarrely enough called *Aeroport*, and next to one of the main arterial roads into the city centre. Collectively, and with the help of the British Embassy, we made an appeal which we were later told went right to the top, but to no avail. In fact the rumour which the interpreter had heard was correct and the area has now been developed as an up-market housing complex. We knew that Aeroflot would oppose any operation out of what they considered *their* airport at Sheremetyevo, which was also Transaero's base, so the idea never saw the light of day.

During one of these visits, we were told that the governor of the Krasnodar Region was interested in buying a couple of 146s, because he felt that the service to Moscow from the resort town of Sochi on the Black Sea was inadequate and unreliable. Sochi was the favourite summer holiday destination for the senior communist party leaders and anyone else who could find a room there, in the days of the Soviet Union, but with foreign travel now so much easier for Russians, it had been forsaken. Nevertheless, there was still plenty of traffic between there and Moscow and indeed other cities and the governor felt that it deserved better services.

After our first meeting, which took place at Sochi's Adler airport, the governor took me to one side and said "I want to show you something." This turned out to be the half-finished front of the terminal building. Apparently, grand plans had been drawn up for a new building and much of the work had been completed to the satisfaction of all concerned, however the money for the work had originally been allocated in the times of the Communist regime and this money was no longer available. Requests to Russian banks had apparently fallen on deaf ears.

"Would you be able to help me?" he asked. I knew that BAe would not get involved in this, but in the post-Communist era, a bank had recently been set up in London called the European Bank for Reconstruction and Development (EBRD), whose remit was to lend money to the newly-emerging countries of the Soviet Bloc. I promised to speak to them when I returned to the UK and take a sounding as to what they might be able to do, the *quid pro quo* being that I felt if I could help him to finish his airport, he would be more amenable to buying our aircraft rather than anyone else's.

A few weeks later I was back in Sochi, armed with route studies and all the usual paraphernalia which we needed. I had spoken to the EBRD and they had expressed cautious interest, though naturally they wanted to know a lot more about it and since I was going out there again, could I ask a few questions for them? We went through the aviation business and then turned to civil engineering. It seemed that the building had been constructed by a Slovenian company who, understandably, had quickly moved out once the money had stopped flowing. On my return, I gave the information to the EBRD, who assured me they would investigate further.

Of course, I began to wonder where, if they could not afford the money to finish the terminal building, would the money come from to buy some new jets? A few diligent enquiries later, I discovered that in fact the Russian banks were willing to back his plans for the airline, but not for the terminal building. Central planning is not something I have ever tried to understand! In the meantime, we received a request for a demonstration, so we went through the motions of organising how and when we would get the aircraft to them. It seemed that my colleagues were planning a demonstration to Air Malta in the near future, followed by one in Turkey, so as demo flights went, it was not too much of a stretch to take it to Sochi. The only problem would be that everyone would require visas and this would take time to set up.

The demo was arranged for July. It was 1994 – five years since the wall had come down and there had been many changes in Russia. Life was now much easier and new buildings were springing up everywhere, including Sochi where a new Radisson hotel had opened. Thus we had a base with good communications, decent food, devoid of cockroaches and next to the Black Sea – bliss!

The governor called me on the morning of the demo to ask what time the flight was arriving. I said it would be early evening because of the Malta demo and the need to refuel, probably in Istanbul. Shortly after this, I received a telex giving the flight details and an ETA and passed on the information. I went down to the airport early, to make sure everything was set up.

I arrived to find lots of people, vehicles and cameras. It transpired that the whole thing was going to be shown live on local TV. I had no way of warning the team – we just had to cross our fingers and hope everything would be OK. The aircraft was marshalled up to the prime spot on the ramp, a red carpet was laid out and two ladies in local costume appeared with a large loaf of bread and some salt, a traditional greeting apparently, to the consternation of all concerned. Usually when you arrive to do a demo there's just you and the handling agent initially. We needn't have worried. Everything went well, the flight crew were interviewed, the governor made a statement and then did his political bit, at which point we left for the hotel.

Later, we went through the plans for the following day. We were to be filmed again, but not live this time – it would appear on the evening news bulletin. The governor had specifically asked if we could do some low flights over Sochi with the cameraman filming from the windows. The demo crews were used to this sort of thing and the 146 was particularly adept at flying low and slow, so they agreed to do it. One thing which we hadn't accounted for, however, was the cabin staff. The boys at Woodford had 'borrowed' two young ladies from the Swiss carrier Crossair, who already had a fleet of 146s, which was fine in itself, but neither of them spoke Russian, so we were going to have to take an interpreter along as well. Fortunately, the lady we had with us had worked on the 125 demos and was familiar with aircraft galleys and how to serve whisky and champagne!

Demo day dawned and being July, the weather was perfect. We set off, doing a run along the line of the Caucasus, which rise immediately behind Sochi and then turned back towards the town and the Hotel Zhemchuzhina (Pearl) which was the pride of the town at the time, perhaps because, for a short time it was one of the biggest hotels in the world with more than 800 rooms.

Shortly afterwards we landed back at Sochi, having at the request of the governor, done a low pass and an orbit of the airport. In those days, Sochi was not a busy airport, so we were not in anyone's way. An hour later, and interviews had taken place, hands had been shaken and the 146 was ready to head back to Istanbul. I stayed behind for further meetings with the governor, who invited me for a meeting at 1100 the following day.

I duly turned up with my briefcase and was shown into his office, but he said "You can leave that here – you won't be needing that where we're going," which immediately had me wondering what he had in mind. We went downstairs to the terminal area, got into one of the Gaz minibuses, and began to head to the other side of the airfield, where a number of helicopters were parked. I noticed there was activity around one of them and we pulled up alongside.

I had been in Russian helicopters before and my abiding memory of them was how noisy they were and how they vibrated when the engines were on full throttle. Much as I was not looking forward too much to this experience, it would be undiplomatic to pull out at this stage, so I boarded the large 12-seat Mil helicopter, along with a number of other people and we took off. Initially, we began to follow the line of the Caucasus and I thought that perhaps we were heading to Krasnodar, the capital of the region. However, it soon became apparent that we were heading inland amongst the mountains.

We landed on one of the few flat pieces of land, about the size of a tennis court, then we were led towards a large yurt, in which there was a fire and a buffet had been prepared. I was glad of the fire, because being summer it was about 30C in Sochi and definitely short-sleeve weather, whereas there was still snow lying at the altitude we had reached.

The food was delicious – I never did find out how they got it up there – and there was much toasting with vodka, so that I remember little of the flight back, but all in all an unusual experience and one that made a change from the usual sort of business trip.

On another visit to Moscow I was invited back at short notice, but I was able to fit in the visit. I was met at the airport, but not by the person I had been dealing with. He was a man I had not met before, but who clearly knew who I was. He explained that the governor was no longer in that position and that it was unlikely that they would proceed with any purchase. He thanked me profusely for my help in pulling together the necessary parties to discuss how best to complete the terminal building work. Apparently some sort of draft contract was being drawn up and work was expected to commence within a few months.

What happened to the governor? I have no idea. Even in the days of *glasnost* it wasn't always wise to ask too many questions. I did make a few enquiries thorough other channels but I never got an answer. My best guess is that he was removed in some sort of local political coup or that he had been found guilty of some mis-demeanour or other and removed from office – not an unusual occurrence at the time.

So the final score was Terminal Building 1, British Aerospace nil – with the referee apparently being sent off.

Since then, the sleepy town of Sochi – even in mid-summer it always seemed surprisingly quiet – has become known all over the world for the Winter Olympics and a Formula 1 circuit. I could never have imagined that 20 years previously.

THE End

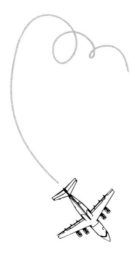